The 21st Century
ENTREPRENEUR

HOW TO START A FREELANCE CONSULTING BUSINESS

JACQUELINE K. POWERS

A Third Millennium Press Book

AVON BOOKS ◆ NEW YORK

AVON BOOKS, INC.
1350 Avenue of the Americas
New York, New York 10019

Copyright © 1999 by Third Millennium Press, Inc., Stephen M. Pollan, and
Jacqueline K. Powers
Cover illustration by Nick Gaetano
Published by arrangement with Third Millennium Press, Inc.
ISBN: 0-380-79712-7
www.avonbooks.com

Library of Congress Cataloging in Publication Data:
Powers, Jacqueline K.
How to start a freelance consulting business / Jacqueline K. Powers.
p.   cm — (The 21st century entrepreneur)
"A Third Millennium Press book."
Includes index.
1. Business consultants. 2. Consultants. 3. Career changes.
4. New business enterprises—Management. 5. Entrepreneurship.
I. Title. II. Series.
HD69.C6P65   1999   99-29549
001'.068—dc21   CIP

First Avon Books Trade Paperback Printing: October 1999

AVON TRADEMARK REG. U.S. PAT. OFF. AND IN OTHER COUNTRIES, MARCA REGISTRADA, HECHO
EN U.S.A.

Printed in the U.S.A.

OPM   10   9   8   7   6   5   4   3   2   1

HOW TO START A FREELANCE CONSULTING BUSINESS

Other **21st CENTURY ENTREPRENEUR** *Titles*
from Avon Books

CONTENTS

HOW TO START A FREELANCE CONSULTING BUSINESS

INTRODUCTION

The world and the workplace are changing, but that's not exactly news. What is news is they're changing in surprising ways—ways that have significance for millions of Americans, including you and me. And these changes in the fabric of our work world are being fueled by several demographic and economic trends that are converging at once.

First trend: Americans are living longer and healthier than ever before, and they are choosing to remain active and productive far longer—well into their senior years. Many aren't interested in the leisure-laden concept of retirement once considered the standard lifetime goal. The idea of days, weeks, and years spent shopping, visiting grandchildren, wandering aimlessly like exiles across the United States in recreational vehicles and tromping across fairways in endless pursuit of dimpled white balls and diminishing handicaps bores many.

These healthy, productive adults have spent years making it as professionals in the workplace. They've gained skills, expertise, and even wisdom over those years, as executives and managers. They love what they do, and they do it well. What they do, in part, defines who they are. They want to continue their work as long as they choose, and as long as they are able.

Second trend: The business climate for skilled professionals has changed, potentially threatening their productivity and career advancement. Once these professionals were assured a long, ladderlike career with a patriarchal, caring employer, or the opportunity to leverage their professional skills and career advancement through keen competition for experienced professionals among the nation's businesses. But the era of downsizing and outsourcing of noncore business functions has decimated the once sacrosanct professional ranks. Businesses have been run with tunnel vision focused myopically on the bottom line, and in order to achieve savings and placate hungry stockholders managers are cutting bodies like kids playing paper dolls.

But the paper dolls are made of flesh and blood, not paper, and the human toll has been horrendous. Bankers, lawyers, accountants, engineers, human resource directors, art directors, and a host of others have walked into work one day only to be handed a pink slip and shown the door. The shock to the ego and the pocketbook is enormous and potentially deadly. Where do you look for a $50,000-a-year job or a $100,000 job or a $200,000 job when businesses across the country are all cutting those same jobs for the same reasons?

The answer is trend number three: You don't go looking for another job; instead, you take advantage of the outsourcing craze to establish your own freelance consulting business. You've got years of experience and expertise on your résumé, so why not twist the villainy of downsizing and outsourcing into an opportunity for personal entrepreneurial success? Perhaps you can even enlist your former employer as your first client.

In truth, there couldn't be a more propitious time for enterprising professionals with entrepreneurial skills to start their own freelance consulting businesses. The consultancy field is growing by leaps and bounds, and business managers say they intend to continue contracting with more and more consultants in the years to come.

The growth in recent years of telecommunications and information technology has made it not only possible, but often relatively easy, for entrepreneurs to establish their businesses inexpensively. Statistics show that more and more savvy entrepreneurs are basing operations in their homes, for a variety of excellent reasons, including cost and flexibility.

Whatever your initial motivation in picking up this book— whether you were the victim of downsizing and felt you had nowhere else to turn, or whether you're simply burned out working long hours for someone else, on their terms instead of your own—

you've come to the right place. This is a nuts-and-bolts book about how to start your own freelance consulting business. I'll cover everything you need to know to get started, from how to decide whether entrepreneurship is for you and how to promote your business, to how to deal with difficult clients and keep them coming back. With all the details in between.

Need a business plan? I'll give you an outline and a sample plan. The same with a marketing plan, and a shopping list for equipping an effective office. By the time you've finished Chapter 1 you'll know whether you've got the right stuff for starting your own consulting business—whether you're really entrepreneur material. By the time you've finished the book you'll probably already have your feet firmly planted on the road to success.

So, bon voyage and best of luck. And don't forget to have fun on your journey.

Part One

•

GETTING STARTED

1

MAKING THE
BIG DECISION

re you a white-collar professional or manager worried about
whether you'll have a job next week, thanks to the mania
for downsizing raging through corporate America? Or, are you
under-challenged—perhaps plain bored—and wishing your job
would just disappear overnight? Maybe you've been racing along
the fast track so furiously you weren't on hand to help baby take
her first steps. Or attend her First Communion. Or watch her win
the state cross-country championship.

If your white collar is beginning to wilt under the sweat and
stress of what's happening in your workplace—for whatever reason—it might be time to dump your job before it swamps you
and to strike out on your own. That's right, start your own business. And what better business for you to start than a freelance
consulting business, in which clients pay you healthy fees to provide them with the distilled essence of all the wisdom you have
accumulated in your years of experience?

Actually, "strike out" is the wrong phrase to use here. We're
really talking about hitting a home run. Maybe even a grand slam.
That's because for many people, becoming an entrepreneur—being
your own boss and being totally responsible for your own income
and career—is exactly the right move to make to ensure you're a
winner in today's career game.

By now it seems all too clear that downsizing isn't merely a
fad. In the past ten years, Fortune 500 companies alone have laid
off close to five million people. Downsizing and restructuring, the

experts say, are here to stay—a permanent part of the economic landscape.

But there's a silver lining to this cloud for those of you who are closet entrepreneurs just waiting for a nudge. Downsizing has created profitable opportunities for freelance consulting businesses. And, ironically enough, often the first place a company will turn to when looking for a consultant is the person who was downsized. After all, who knows the business better than the professional who just left it?

As more and more companies slash and burn divisions in order to focus their resources and energy on their core business— whether it's manufacturing widgets or selling pharmaceuticals— they are looking to outsiders to take over their noncore functions. For most businesses, labor remains the biggest expense, and one managers eye immediately when talk turns to cost cutting. As salary and benefits packages for employees continue to rise, the financial allure of hiring outside consultants, whose fees are fixed and temporary, also rises.

Businesses today are outsourcing everything from marketing, sales, communications, and public relations, to personnel issues, financial management, and information technology. And as a result, the opportunities for savvy entrepreneurs to start freelance consulting businesses are flourishing.

At the same time, the lure and acceptance of home-based businesses has grown. Currently there are twenty million home-based businesses nationwide, according to IDC/LINK, a New York— based market research firm. That number is growing annually by 7 to 8 percent, and is expected to reach almost thirty million by 2001. Already, when you include telecommuters who work for someone else, there are 30 million U.S. households in which someone works at home, 33 percent more than in 1992.

While you don't have to base your freelance consulting business at home, it is a great way to keep start-up costs down. As the price of sophisticated technology and equipment has dropped, home-based freelance consulting has become one of the most affordable ways to fulfill the dream of owning your own business. By spending as little as $4,000 to $14,000, you can enter a business in which the top practitioners earn more than $300,000 a year. Remember, you and the marketplace determine what you can charge clients for your services. But as a business owner you alone—by dint of your energy, skill, enthusiasm, and inclination—determine what your future income will be.

WHAT ARE THE ADVANTAGES?

The worldwide consultancy market is estimated to employ 100,000 experts, and earns $40 billion a year—$15 billion to $18 billion of that in the United States, up from $4 billion in 1985. The Gartner Group expects income from management consulting fees to double by the year 2000. That's a huge chunk of change, and one you can tap into. But before you let dollar signs dazzle you into a hasty decision, consider the pros and cons of starting your own home-based, freelance consulting business.

You determine your fate

When you work for yourself, you are master of your fate. You determine your own future and your future income. That can be an exhilarating thought, but also may send chills down your spine. A little of both is reasonable, but later in this chapter you'll take an Entrepreneurial Aptitude Test to determine whether you've got the right stuff for striking out on your own. If the test shows that in your case the chills outweigh the thrills, you'll know to sit tight or look for employment elsewhere.

But for many of you, being your own boss—no longer at the mercy of a soulless, impersonal, indifferent corporation—would be a definite advantage.

The price is right

If you decide to base your business at home, the price is right indeed. You can spend as little as $4,000 to get started, if you buy used computer equipment or if you already own good equipment. What you're selling is stored inside your brain—your wisdom and years of work experience—so you have no rent, no inventory, and little or no overhead. You can convert your basement to a home office, print up business cards on your computer, and voilà—you're off and running.

You'll also save money by cutting out the little things you've been spending money on when you go to the office every day. No more parking and commuter costs and lunches out. You can cut way down on costly business attire, too. Most people who work at home dress casually, at least most of the time. Some actually confess to working in the buff, but of course that's a personal choice, entirely up to you.

You can better balance work and family

Many people who work at home actually find they spend more hours, more productively, on the job. After all, when your office is right down the hall from your bedroom you can put all that former commuting time to work productively. In fact, according to research by Paul and Sarah Edwards, authors of *Working from Home* (Tarcher/Putnam), people who are successfully self-employed at home work an average of sixty-one hours a week.

Being self-employed means having more control over your life, and being better able to balance work and family lives. And you have more flexibility because you set your work schedule and workload instead of your boss, which means that if you prefer not to work afternoons in the summer so you can attend you son's swimming meets, or hit the golf course, or take a marketing seminar, that's fine. You can make up the time at 9 P.M. or work Saturday morning. Or not. It's up to you.

On the other hand, if you like, you can send off a sales letter while catching up on the progress of the Ryder Cup on TV. Or throw in a load of wash while taking a break from the computer.

You also can be as accessible to your friends and clients as you choose. You can set strict working hours and specific visiting or playing hours, or you can go with the flow. Again, it's your choice and you can do what's best for you. If you work for yourself you can actually heed the call of your own biorhythms, rather than contorting yourself to the dictates of a boss's decision. And if you prefer to work with your favorite music playing in the background, that's fine, too.

Many women, particularly those who have struggled to reach the highest ranks of corporate management, are now opting out of the corporate fast track in favor of starting their own businesses at home. Today 37 percent of small businesses are owned by women, and a good percentage of those are based at home. Many women are making that choice so Mom can be there when the kids come home from school—at least to say "Hi" and "How are you, honey?" before firmly closing the office door and turning the kids' care over to a cherished housekeeper. They've learned that women today can have the best of both worlds, and do it on their own terms.

You can fashion the perfect work environment

When you decide to work at home, you have the freedom and pleasure of working in an environment you can design to suit your individual needs. And it's already in a larger environment in which you feel comfortable, because it's home. At home you'll be able to open a window and breathe fresh air instead of stale, recirculated, institutional carbon dioxide.

Esthetically, your new work environment can be more pleasing. If you want to hang family photos and artwork on the walls, there's no one to stop you and no need to consider whether the "look" of your office space is sufficiently professional—unless, of course, you intend to meet with clients there. Contrast this warm, homey feel to large, impersonal office buildings or small, sterile, strip mall offices, and already your creative and problem-solving juices will be flowing more freely.

And better yet, you don't have to drive yourself bananas getting there. Just think, you'll never again confront that nerve-racking, gut-wrenching, twice-daily grind called commuting. When your business is in your home, you're already there when other frenzied businesspeople—commuters—are tearing their hair out on the expressway or elbowing their way to a seat on the train. You can even turn over and go back to bed for another hour or so, if that's what you feel like doing. After all, it's your business and you're already there.

You can revel in the pride of ownership

Sure, you've felt a sense of accomplishment every time you've successfully completed a project at work over the years. Or when you've made exactly the right decision for the company. And if your bosses have been good ones they've dealt out a fair share of praise, congratulations, and even bonuses over the years.

But there's absolutely nothing like the sense of pride and self-satisfaction you can justifiably feel when you nail a new client for yourself, successfully finish a project for that client, and then hear he's delighted with your work and will be calling on you again soon. Nothing, that is, except when you look at your accounting ledger and your bank account and realize that you, and you alone, are bringing in the bucks by operating your own business based on your brain and skill and talent alone.

THERE ARE DISADVANTAGES, TOO

Starting your own home-based consulting business sounds like a sure-fire secret to success right about now. But you should be aware that there are downsides to consider, and many of them are the flip side of the advantages I just listed.

You and you alone determine your fate

If that thought scares you, think twice before you leap into business ownership. Going it alone really isn't for everyone. Not only can it be a rat race, always racing for your next client, but it can be very lonely, as well. You may miss the warmth, companionship, and even support of the workplace environment. You won't have coworkers to act as sounding boards for your latest idea or as focus groups for your newest project. Or even just to take a break with around the water cooler and exchange personal gossip. And don't forget you won't be drawing a guaranteed salary.

The price may not be right

You'll need to invest some money in your venture and that entails some risk. If it turns out you can't generate sufficient income in your new business, you'll lose your investment, or at least part of it. Worse, you might end up with some new debts. Depending on your current situation, you should ask yourself if you're ready to bet your financial stability on the dream of business ownership.

As a business consultant you sell yourself. And as a freelance business consultant you will have to sell yourself not just once, to an employer, but over and over and over again, to each new client. It'll get easier as time goes on and you build your track record and your stable of satisfied clients willing to offer testimonials to your expertise, but you still have to close the next deal and the one after that. It can be exhausting and ultimately not worth the personal cost.

It can be hard to juggle work and family

Greater flexibility. Your schedule's entirely your own, with your office right down the hall. Softer lighting, homier ambiance. Sounds great, right? Maybe not. If your aim is to better balance family and work, as in find more time to spend with your spouse and kids, establishing your own business may be the wrong move.

That's because most entrepreneurs, even those who work at home, end up working longer hours than they did when they were employed by someone else. And as the boss, you're restricting your life in many ways. Let's face it, the boss just can't call in sick when he or she wants to and assume someone else will pick up the slack. You can't disappoint your clients too often without losing them.

And unless you're incredibly self-disciplined, that flexibility and proximity can work against you. If you're a workaholic it may be hard to break away from the computer even at 3 A.M. when an idea strikes. And if you tend to be more easily distracted, by the sound of your children playing outside your office window or the lure of CNN *Headline News,* you may find it harder to stick to business in that homier atmosphere.

Regardless of the advantages and disadvantages of starting your own freelance consulting business, being an entrepreneur just isn't for everyone.

DO YOU HAVE WHAT IT TAKES?

You've considered the pros and cons of starting your own free-lance consulting business and decided the pros seem to outweigh the cons. What's next? That phrase "seem to" in the previous sentence is critical. The next step is to determine whether you really have what it takes to become a successful entrepreneur.

First you'll do a complete attitudinal self-checkup so you don't rush blindly down the wrong path. Whether you've been down-sized out of your management job or are just looking to make a change—for whatever reason—you need to determine what kind of career move is best for you. We don't want to assume that starting your own consulting business is the right step. Maybe you really would prefer to return to your old job or a similar one. How about changing careers? Should you take advantage of new, more flexible scheduling options at someone else's business? Remember, your career options are still open.

Before making your next professional move, you need to answer the following questions to figure out exactly where your interests lie. After that, we'll analyze the eight key traits of the successful entrepreneur. Then, finally, you can round out the decision-making process by taking the Entrepreneurial Aptitude Test.

Remember, your answers to the following questions will begin to build the foundation for your future. You need to do it right, and that means you need to begin building what will become, in addition to this book, your business bible. This may sound simplis-tic to an experienced professional like you, but you'd be amazed how many people, when starting out on a totally new course, forget the basics.

Go out now to your nearest office supply store and purchase an oversize, heavy-duty, three-ring binder. Over the coming months it will become both your resource and your guide. Get a good supply of paper and a couple packages of dividers—there are many different areas we'll need to cover as we get ready to launch your business.

If you have a personal computer and a good printer, set up an electronic file, if you prefer. But be sure to print out the answers to these questions and the other plans you make as we go along, and put those into your notebook, too. It's going to be important for you to be able to carry that notebook wherever you go. You'll want to place it by your bed each night, because chances are you'll be waking at 2 A.M., excited by an idea you'll want to jot down immediately so that you don't forget it.

It's important to start your notebook now, then answer these questions. And be honest in your answers. This is one case where you'll truly only hurt yourself and jeopardize your future success if you fudge even a little bit.

☛ QUESTIONS TO ASK YOURSELF

What are my interests?

Did I enjoy my last job?

Did I hate my last job but enjoy my field or business?

Did any of my coworkers or friends in another field have the kind of job I dreamed of?

What kinds of activities or subjects interest me most?

Do I like analyzing a problem and finding solutions?

Do I know how to find information and answers to questions I can't answer?

Do I like sharing what I know?

What kind of work environment do I want?

Do I want to be physically active or sedentary and cerebrally active?

Do I want to spend most of my time indoors or outdoors?

Do I want to continue living where I am now?

Do I want to work with other people or by myself?

Do I want to work with a large group of people, many different kinds of people, or a small, homogeneous group?

What kind of people would I like to have as coworkers? Clients?

What work hours and work schedule would I most like to have?

Do I need to work full or part time?

Would I like to travel in my job?

What is my career goal?

Do I need the salary and benefits I currently have or had? Could I earn enough in some other field?

How much money do I need or want to earn?

Would I be willing to invest my time and money in the necessary training or retraining to make a radical change?

What are the major reasons I would seek a change?

Do I want to work for myself or someone else?

Do I want to work for my former or current boss?

Would my former employer be willing to hire me back on a more flexible or reduced work schedule?

Do I prefer to be my own boss?

Do I have unique and marketable ideas, knowledge, and skills?

Am I willing to take a risk with some of my savings?

Am I willing to assume the full burden of responsibility for a business?

Do I have sufficient financial resources to start a business?

Answer these questions honestly, then take a good look at your answers. They will help you come to a better understanding of yourself and where you should be heading in your career. Chances are if you bought this book your gut instincts are correct and you're mentally ready to begin the process of establishing your own consulting business. But first you need to be sure you understand what it takes to be a successful entrepreneur.

The Road Warrior

So what are the key qualities of a successful entrepreneur? I like to visualize Mel Gibson in *The Road Warrior*. Or if you're an old movie buff, think about John Wayne in just about any movie he made. Visualize the Road Warrior, a tough-guy hero who makes it all happen and happen right. Got the picture? Take a mental snapshot and let's talk about this guy for a minute. What exactly is he like? What are his key traits?

Confidence. Probably the first thing you notice is confidence. This guy or gal exudes confidence from every pore. He straddles the highway or corral looking ten feet tall, with the air of someone who can easily defeat the bad guys without ever firing a single shot. Chin up, he looks you squarely in the eye, shoulders straight and set, watchful yet at ease. He's ready to take on the world and win. He is, in short, a winner and he knows it. To be a successful entrepreneur you have to believe in yourself, believe unflinchingly you can do it.

Drive. Nothing, but nothing, stopped Mel Gibson in *The Road Warrior*. Not the Humongous and his entire army of bad guys, not an arsenal of weapons. Because the Road Warrior has drive, and his natural energy fuels that drive. He's driven by his mission. He's single-minded and committed to his goal and marches relentlessly toward victory. That energy and drive are essential for the successful entrepreneur.

Determination. And just as the entrepreneur's natural energy fuels his drive, that drive fuels his determination. Despite setbacks, Mel Gibson and John Wayne never seriously falter in their march to victory. They set their square jaws and persist, refusing to let stumbling blocks deflect them from their path. Instead they consider each problem carefully and devise a solution, always with their eye on their main goal. They can do anything they set their minds to. It's just a question of making the mental commitment, of digging in their heels and deciding to do it, and doing it right.

Integrity. Picture John Wayne straddling a town's single dusty street in front of the swinging doors of the saloon. Look into his eyes. You know instantly that whatever else you might discover about this man, he's a man of integrity. He's a man you can trust with your life, if it should come to that. A personal integrity that shines through all your actions is key to becoming a successful entrepreneur. When you own your own business, clients look into your eyes and no one else's to decide whether to entrust their business to you. They want to be assured that you're honest and honorable and trustworthy—in short, that you are a person of integrity.

Experience. You don't have to know all the answers. This isn't really a movie, after all, and even Mel Gibson doesn't have all the answers. But few green, unseasoned warriors have what it takes to succeed in their own business, particularly a consulting business. To be a successful entrepreneur you need those years in the field to help you overcome the obstacles that will inevitably fall in your path. This is one of the secrets of your future success. You're an experienced expert in your field. Now you can distill that experience and those skills you've honed and put them to use in your own business.

Common sense. Hand in hand with experience goes common sense. As an entrepreneur you need to stay grounded in reality, like John Wayne's characters. Those guys stayed alive by knowing instinctively when to duck, when to check their backs, and when to shoot first. Common sense is about trusting your instincts, about knowing where to find the answers to questions you can't answer, and about not relying on pat formulas and rote learning. As a beginning entrepreneur, when the going gets tough or you make a mistake, chances are you won't find the solution in a textbook for Business Management 101. The best solution is probably right in your head, simply waiting for you to figure it out.

Creativity. You may think Mel Gibson's Road Warrior an unlikely source of creativity, but think again. The Road Warrior survived by finding food and fuel in a burned out, desert landscape. And he patched and protected and armed his vehicle by using common, everyday household items creatively. Common sense and experience are essential for the budding entrepreneur, but they'll take you only so far.

Creativity means thinking new thoughts, having new ideas, going beyond the known to the unknown and transforming it—harnessing it. To be successful you'll need creativity to find just the right way to market your skills most effectively to bring in clients.

Flexibility. Finally, Mel Gibson's Road Warrior had to be flexible, and so do you if you intend to make it as an entrepreneur. If an idea or plan doesn't work, you can't let yourself waste time, energy, and emotion bemoaning that failure. You need to be able to learn from failure and quickly come up with an alternative method. You have to be adaptable and throw your ego out the door, so you can continue to move forward when things don't go quite as you expected. While you'll need to stay focused to achieve your goal, you may need to try several different means to get there in the end.

For example, one marketing approach may work for a while and then stall. At that point you'll need to be flexible and come up with something new. Remember, every business plan and every business can benefit from a fresh look and a few minor adjustments every once in a while, even if things seem to be going just right.

So now you've got a good snapshot of what an entrepreneur looks like, and how that translates into the key character traits necessary for a successful entrepreneur. It's time to find out, once and for all, if you're really entrepreneurial material. If you have what it takes to start up and make a success of your own consulting business. Sharpen your pencil, get out your business notebook, and start a new section labeled, "Making of an Entrepreneur."

First, draw a line down the center of one sheet of paper to create two columns. Label one column "Pros," the other "Cons." Then number and list the pros I enumerated earlier in this chapter and add your own. Do the same for cons.

On a second sheet of paper, write, "Entrepreneurial Character Traits" on the top line. Make two vertical columns, one column headed "Entrepreneur," the other column "Me." In the first column, list the eight entrepreneurial character traits I mentioned earlier. In the second column list your own key personality traits.

Finally, on a third piece of paper copy down the questions in the test below. Then answer them carefully and thoughtfully. Remember, be honest. There are no right or wrong answers, but there are pitfalls and wrong paths, and honest answers to this test will help you avoid them.

Entrepreneurial Aptitude Test

1. I would readily give up my golf league, weekends, evenings, and most leisure-time activities for a year or two to start my own business and get it running properly.
   A. strongly agree
   B. moderately agree
   C. moderately disagree
   D. strongly disagree

2. I've found over the years that I'm more determined than most people and can do just about anything I set my mind to.
   A. strongly agree
   B. moderately agree
   C. moderately disagree
   D. strongly disagree

3. My supervisors and colleagues have said I have a sharp, analytical mind.
   A. strongly agree
   B. moderately agree
   C. moderately disagree
   D. strongly disagree

4. In my previous jobs I worked long, hard hours for extended periods, and I would still be willing and able to do so.
   A. strongly agree
   B. moderately agree
   C. moderately disagree
   D. strongly disagree

5. I've always felt compelled to be the best in everything I do.
   A. strongly agree
   B. moderately agree
   C. moderately disagree
   D. strongly disagree

6. I get frustrated easily.
   A. strongly agree

B. moderately agree
C. moderately disagree
D. strongly disagree

7. At this point in my life I savor a challenge and don't want to waste my time on routine tasks.
   A. strongly agree
   B. moderately agree
   C. moderately disagree
   D. strongly disagree

8. I've learned to value competency over personality and prefer to work with a difficult person who is very competent rather than one who's very congenial but less competent.
   A. strongly agree
   B. moderately agree
   C. moderately disagree
   D. strongly disagree

9. I am usually the one to organize a group of people and take charge.
   A. strongly agree
   B. moderately agree
   C. moderately disagree
   D. strongly disagree

10. I had enough of taking orders in my previous career and never have liked being told what to do.
    A. strongly agree
    B. moderately agree
    C. moderately disagree
    D. strongly disagree

11. I've learned to be efficient and to stick to a strict schedule in order to complete tasks in a timely way.
    A. strongly agree
    B. moderately agree
    C. moderately disagree
    D. strongly disagree

12. I would value my employees' well-being, but not at the expense of my business.
   A. strongly agree
   B. moderately agree
   C. moderately disagree
   D. strongly disagree

13. Given reasonable odds, my efforts usually can successfully influence the outcome of an endeavor.
   A. strongly agree
   B. moderately agree
   C. moderately disagree
   D. strongly disagree

14. My energy level is higher now than it was in my younger years when I sometimes lacked focus, and seems to be higher than that of most people.
   A. strongly agree
   B. moderately agree
   C. moderately disagree
   D. strongly disagree

15. I have seen and encountered a variety of problems over the years, and most things do not fluster or unnerve me.
   A. strongly agree
   B. moderately agree
   C. moderately disagree
   D. strongly disagree

16. I've learned to be patient, that everything takes a certain amount of time and can't be rushed.
   A. strongly agree
   B. moderately agree
   C. moderately disagree
   D. strongly disagree

17. I love the challenge of analyzing, attacking, and completing a complex task.
   A. strongly agree

B. moderately agree
C. moderately disagree
D. strongly disagree

18. In both my previous career and in my personal life I've often led and directed projects and groups.
    A. strongly agree
    B. moderately agree
    C. moderately disagree
    D. strongly disagree

19. I tend to be somewhat inflexible, and find it difficult to change course once I've started a project, even if it begins to look as though success is unlikely.
    A. strongly agree
    B. moderately agree
    C. moderately disagree
    D. strongly disagree

20. I know I'm capable of firing an unproductive employee, although I wouldn't be happy at the prospect of doing it.
    A. strongly agree
    B. moderately agree
    C. moderately disagree
    D. strongly disagree

21. I like to experiment and try new things—from wine, to food, to meeting new people and trying new activities.
    A. strongly agree
    B. moderately agree
    C. moderately disagree
    D. strongly disagree

22. I have had how many year(s) of experience in the field in which I plan to start a business.
    A. zero
    B. one-half to one
    C. one to two
    D. more than two

23. I've had the following business experience:
  A. five to ten years in a management position in a success-
     ful firm
  B. five to ten years in a management position in any firm
  C. less than five years of management experience

24. I've been ill to the extent that it curtailed my activities for
how many days over the past three years.
  A. zero to five
  B. six to ten
  C. eleven to fifteen
  D. sixteen or above

25. I function most effectively if I get at least how many hours
of sleep a night.
  A. eight
  B. seven
  C. six
  D. five or less

Scoring your answers

Now, check the answer you marked down and see how many
points it's worth. Put that number next to your answer. When
you're finished you're going to total your score, then find out just
what it suggests about your chances of becoming a successful
entrepreneur.

  1. Need for leisure—entrepreneurs are willing to forgo a lifestyle
     based on leisure (a=4, b=3, c=2, d=1)
  2. Self-confidence—an obvious necessity (a=4, b=3, c=2, d=1)
  3. Conceptual ability—successful entrepreneurs are stars at this
     (a=4, b=3, c=2, d=1)
  4. Energy level—it must be high (a=4, b=3, c=2, d=1)
  5. Need for achievement, as opposed to status (a=4, b=3,
     c=2, d=1)
  6. Emotional stability—the more stable the better (a=1, b=2, c=
     3, d=4)

7. Attraction to challenge, opportunity—otherwise, why start your own business? (a=4, b=3, c=2, d=1)
8. Objective approach to interpersonal relationships—entrepreneurs sometimes have to regard people as a means to an end (a=4, b=3, c=2, d=1)
9. Need for power—a strong one is essential (a=4, b=3, c=2, d=1)
10. Need for power (a=4, b=3, c=2, d=1)
11. Sense of urgency—a powerful one is a prerequisite (a=4, b=3, c=2, d=1)
12. Objective approach to interpersonal relationships (a=4, b=3, c=2, d=1)
13 Internal locus of control—believing you control your own destiny—a must for successful entrepreneurs (a=4, b=3, c=2, d=1)
14. Energy level (a=4, b=3, c=2, d=1)
15. Emotional stability (a=4, b=3, c=2, d=1)
16. Sense of urgency (a=1, b=2, c=3, d=4)
17. Conceptual ability (a=4, b=3, c=2, d=1)
18. Leadership skills (a=4, b=3, c=2, d=1)
19. Realism and flexibility—entrepreneurs cannot be rigid when seeking solutions to problems (a=1, b=2, c=3, d=4)
20. Objective approach to interpersonal relationships (a=4, b=3, c=2, d=1)
21. The most successful entrepreneurs are open to new experiences, opportunities, and challenges—they like to try new things (a=4, b=3, c=2, d=1)
22. The more business experience the better (a=1, b=2, c=3, d=4)
23. Five to ten years in a management position in a successful company is the best experience to prepare you to succeed as an entrepreneur (a=4, b=3, c=1)
24. Regardless of age, the healthier you are the more you will be able to handle the stress and long hours that come with entrepreneurship (a=4, b=3, c=2, d=1)
25. Energy level (a=1, b=2, c=3, d=4)

What Your Score Means

Add up your total score, then check out where your score falls in the categories below. If you score 85 or above, you're on your way and it's clear sailing. If you scored below 85 . . . well, read on.

94–100: What are you waiting for? You possess most, if not all, of the key personality and behavioral traits of the entrepreneur. You have the best chance to succeed.

85–93: Go for it! You possess most of the characteristics of an entrepreneur. If your score on the last five questions was 23 or above, your behavioral attitudes could compensate for any personality traits you are lacking.

75–84: Think again. You possess some entrepreneurial traits but probably not to the degree necessary to buck the daunting odds and be successful. If your score on the last five questions was 22 or below, the risk is even greater. Remember, entrepreneurs are not attracted to risk, they are attracted to challenge and opportunities. You might consider working for someone else—you probably aren't cut out to be an entrepreneur.

Below 75: Stay right where you are. Your personality traits and behavior patterns suggest you work better in a corporate environment.

So now you've taken the Entrepreneurial Aptitude Test. Remember, whether you passed or failed, the test is only a guide. It's not foolproof. Only you can answer the question of whether you're truly an entrepreneur.

Even if you failed the test, if you are determined enough you can learn to run your own business successfully.

So, look into your own heart—do you like what you see? Do you feel strongly that, at least partly thanks to your years of experience and character building, you are entrepreneurial material? If so, then you, with the help of this book, are ready to become the master of your business future.

My friend Lynda Ford didn't have this book to guide her when she started her own freelance human resources consulting business, The Ford Group, a year ago in Utica, New York. She didn't take the Entrepreneurial Aptitude test or the attitudinal self-checkup, but she knew she wasn't happy working as an employee. In addition, the challenge had faded from the job and she wanted a more flexible schedule to be able to spend more time with her two teenage boys.

"I had this awful feeling of dread going to work every day. I know what I want, and I really chafe at working for other people," Ford said.

Her husband, Greeley, earns a good living, and they had been socking some money away with the idea that she might start her own business. So she sort of helped her employer downsize her out of her job.

But like most new businesses, it took a while to get going. "The first six months were very sparse," she said. She earned only a couple thousand dollars in revenue. But she spent at least 50 percent of her time on "marketing, networking, and just plain hobnobbing." Her first client came from word of mouth through her former employer and went away quite satisfied. And spread the word. In her second six months revenue multiplied dramatically, and by the end of her first year she had exceeded her business plan goal of adding a client a month. She now has fifteen and her phone is ringing off the hook.

For now, she said, that's a better measure of her success than dollars. "I'm pleased most of my business is repeat business and referrals. All my first accounts are calling back, and the new calls are referrals from satisfied clients."

Better yet, she's having a ball. "I get up every day and I'm so happy. I think, 'Oh, this is so neat. What calls should I make today, what projects will I work on?' There's an old Chinese proverb that says, 'Find something you love and you'll never work another day in your life.' That's how I feel."

For Lynda, the time was right and so was she. Her hunch and confidence in her own abilities paid off. She made the right move when she started The Ford Group.

TWO CASE STUDIES

Let me introduce you to two people we'll follow throughout this book, as they attempt to start their own freelance management consulting businesses. They're not real people. They're composites drawn from my interviews and discussions with real-life people in preparation for writing this book. But their stories, their mistakes and successes, and their ups and downs can help you avoid pitfalls and guide your path as you embark on your own entrepreneurial adventure.

Meet Monica DuBois

Monica was forty-five when she was fired—not downsized, just plain fired—from her director-level human resources job four years ago. Her firing came as a complete shock, one that left her emotionally and financially devastated.

Monica was used to success—this was the first time in her life she ever failed at anything. Moreover, she was the family's biggest wage earner, earning about $90,000 a year. Her husband, Dan, worked as a photographer for the local university in a job he loved, but earned just $35,000 a year.

That wasn't a problem for either of them. Monica was a Type A personality who loved the challenge and stress of her job, as well as the sense of personal accomplishment the job and salary brought her. And she was happy that her salary allowed Dan the flexibility of staying in the relatively low-paying job he loved. They had a very satisfying lifestyle, and weren't worried about financing college for their two teenagers. They'd established college funds early on, and as long as Monica's salary kept going up, they anticipated no problem. Then their personal earthquake struck.

Here's what happened: Five years ago, Monica was director of human resources for a small community newspaper that was part of a national chain. She loved it. But then a spot as an assistant director at corporate headquarters opened up and the vice president for human resources asked her to take it. That meant a big increase in salary and a major career move, with the possibility of a top-level corporate position down the road.

She and the vice president had always gotten along great. When she interviewed with the director to whom she would report, though, she got a funny feeling. The woman, who was new to the company, was cordial enough, but seemed intent on interviewing others and wasn't sure Monica had the "right experience" for the new position.

The vice president said "Don't worry," and Monica ignored that funny feeling. She got the job. For nine months. Then the vice president jumped to another company, Monica's boss took over as vice president, and shortly thereafter Monica got the boot. When she got over the shock and tears and sense of betrayal— she had worked for the company twenty years, after all—she realized that from the beginning, she had represented a threat to her new boss. There weren't many women in positions of power at the corporate level, and her boss didn't want any competition for advancement. So Monica was out, with a severance package worth about $30,000.

Monica didn't adjust well to what she perceived as her failure. She felt she had to do something fast to generate sufficient income to keep their lifestyle afloat. That's when she started making mistakes.

First, she was so upset over the way she'd been treated she decided she wanted a complete change in her career. And she didn't want to work for anyone else, ever again. So she started reading the "Businesses for Sale" ads in the local newspaper, and within three weeks had spent $20,000 of her severance package on a mailing and packaging business.

Needless to say, she didn't take the time to research the business thoroughly beyond a cursory look at the books. And they didn't paint an accurate picture, to say the least. The business had been run into the ground, lost customer goodwill, accumulated debts, and faced major new competition from a modern post office branch under construction down the road.

But even worse than that, it didn't take more than a few weeks before Monica realized that wrapping up packages for mailing wasn't at all how she wanted to spend the next twenty years of her life. Her business was people, not packages. She'd reacted too quickly to her job loss. She hadn't assessed herself and her personal and career needs, and consequently she'd made a terrible, costly mistake.

It was only after that debacle that she started analyzing herself, her character traits, her likes and dislikes, and her skills and talents. That was when she decided she still loved human resources; she was good at it, and had years of experience to put to good use. One thing didn't change. She still didn't want to work for anyone else, at least not yet. She wanted to try to go it on her own, so she decided to start her own consulting business.

Now, meet Aaron Steinberg

Aaron did things quite differently from Monica. But then, Aaron wasn't fired or downsized. Aaron was very observant and took note of the downsizing fever that was sweeping corporate America. As director of public relations at a moderate-size computer software company, Aaron didn't fear his job would disappear. The company was growing, after all. But, he thought, you never know.

Aaron was the cautious, conservative type. He wanted to be ready in case disaster struck. His wife was a schoolteacher and her job was quite secure. Aaron put them on a very strict household budget and started stashing away a good portion of his wife's income—either for a rainy day . . . or for an opportunity.

Because Aaron had a plan: He thought he might be able to tap into the outsourcing trend that was the flip side of the downsizing trend. He'd always wanted to be his own boss—to start his own P.R. company—but he'd never been able to put together a sufficient cushion to feel comfortable about giving up the safety net of his substantial paycheck.

So Aaron watched, waited, saved what he could in what he called his special entrepreneurial account, and read. He read books about starting your own business, books about starting a home-based business, and books about consulting. And he did something else while he read. He quietly started networking and put out feelers for projects he could do on his own, on his own time. He started moonlighting.

He was careful, too, to bid only on jobs too small or inappropriate for his employer. He didn't want to be dishonest with his boss, and he didn't want to be unethical. He decided not to compete with his employer for clients—yet. But the network of contacts he'd made over the years on the job proved invaluable both for leads and clients. One client led to two, then to several. His time and stress level began to pinch, as demand for his services grew.

He considered severing the umbilical cord that tied him to his employer, but decided to wait until his outside work—and entrepreneurial fund—accumulated a cushion equal to a year's salary on the job. There wasn't any real rush to go solo, he decided. Besides, he wanted to do things right.

THE TIME IS RIGHT

Becoming an entrepreneur is a big decision. Perhaps you're still not convinced it's the right step to take. That's okay. It's better to err on the side of caution. But read on, because you can be sure that now is the right time for the right person to start his own freelance consulting business. Large and small companies that have cut to the bone are hiring people just like you—their former managers and professionals—to do for them on a contract basis what they used to do at greater expense in-house. But more about why the time is right for you to start your new business in Chapter 2.

2

THE TIME IS RIGHT

Both economics and demographics are changing the way Americans look at the concepts of work and career. We all want to live the good life, and we're willing to work long and hard for the luxuries that entails. Forget the meatloaf and mashed potatoes life our parents led. Many of us grew up on salmon and sorbets, crostini and crudité. We skied Aspen in winter and spent summers sprawled on the Nantucket sand. Our garages cradled a minimum of two well-waxed autos, at least one of which was a foreign-made, luxury model.

And if that wasn't your life, it's one you aspired to.

You get the picture—we're talking the kind of life you get addicted to, the kind of life you can't even think of giving up. The problem is, you might have to. Or, you may be worried you'll have to. Or that you'll have to find a new way of paying for it.

Say you're vice president for communications at Widgets, Inc. You've been with the company twenty years. You earn a healthy six-figure salary and a bonus. But you're nervous about your job. And with good reason. You've looked to your left, looked to your right, and realized the managers who once occupied the desks next to yours aren't there anymore. Neither are the desks, in fact.

Most companies aren't giving out gold watches anymore. In part that's because many companies no longer have twenty-year employees. And, even more troubling, many companies no longer have communications departments. Those departments and others have gone the way of the dinosaur as U.S. companies flock like lemmings to the downsizing trend that's sliced corporate staffs to the bone and beyond during the 1980s and 1990s. For two decades companies have been cutting all but their core departments and outsourcing everything else. It's a trend experts expect to continue as stockholders and boards of directors continue to peer myopically at the bottom line.

Frankly, it's just not a good time to be an employee, and especially a member of the professional and managerial class.

More than 43 million American jobs have been eliminated since 1979, according to a *New York Times* analysis. While many of those job cuts were the result of normal business cycles, and many other jobs were created during those years, for the first time in the history of corporate America the jobs being cut are not primarily in the blue-collar ranks. Many of the jobs that no longer exist, and which used to feed families of four salmon and sorbet, were in the professional and management ranks.

In the past ten years, Fortune 500 companies alone have laid off close to 5 million people. And many of those 5 million high-wage earners today are facing greatly reduced expectations and family dislocations and disintegration. Many are looking for new jobs at half the salary, if they're lucky. Others have given up looking.

THE DOWNSIZING CLIMATE IS DIFFERENT TODAY

Downsizing itself is nothing new. Businesses have been laying off workers almost since the dawn of time. But downsizing is more pervasive now than at any other time in history, and it means something different to America's workforce, too. Some statistics from that *New York Times* poll, included in a special report, "The Downsizing of America," illustrate the problem. For example:

Nearly three-fourths of all households have "had a close encounter with layoffs since 1980."

In one-third of all households a family member has been laid off, and almost 40 percent more know someone who was laid off.

One in ten adults—about 19 million people, equal to the com-
bined adult populations of New York and New Jersey—admitted a layoff had caused a major crisis in their lives.

Scary, isn't it? And remember: The worker who is being laid
off today, is—you! White-collar, professional American workers
are taking it on the chin and in the workplace, as they never have
before. Unlike the downsizings of the early 1980s, today most
workers being laid off have some college education; according to
the *Times* poll, better-paid workers—those earning at least $50,000
a year—are being laid off at twice the rate they were in the 1980s.
The definition of layoff is also changing. It used to mean putting
an employee out of work, usually temporarily. Most employees
who were laid off, if there was no problem with their performance,
could expect to be rehired. In fact, many layoffs were seasonal.
Now, no such luck. The word *layoff* today should have the word
permanent permanently attached. Your chances of getting rehired
are less than none.

Although permanent layoffs have been symptomatic of most
recessions in the past, today's layoffs are happening at an acceler-
ated rate during an economic recovery that's lasted more than six
years. And they're occurring at companies that are doing very,
very well.

Yet, despite all the layoffs, there's been a net increase of 27
million jobs since 1979. The unemployment rate is the lowest it's
been since 1973, at five percent in June 1997, and companies are
now trying to lure competent workers with all kinds of fringe
benefits, from flextime work schedules to on-site day care. That's
right: Jobs are out there, even for the permanently downsized. So
what's the problem?

TODAY'S JOBS DEMAND MORE, PAY LESS

The problem is, many of today's jobs demand more, pay less, and
offer less challenge and satisfaction than the jobs they've replaced.
In the past, most people who were laid off found similar jobs that
paid as much or more than the job they'd lost. Today, only about

a third of those laid off find new jobs that pay as well or better than their old jobs.

That's because managerial and professional jobs are disappearing at a higher rate today, and many of the new jobs being created are in the service industry. Workers in these new jobs are being trained to perform specific tasks—often in the service of others or to enhance others' lives—rather than being called on to use their brains to create ideas and products and to solve problems.

Economists also say job insecurity has stunted wage growth, despite today's low unemployment rate. Workers are nervous about pressing for higher wages for fear of being laid off. Labor Department statistics show that today's median wage, adjusted for inflation, is almost three percent lower than what it was in 1979. And while average family income rose about 10 percent between 1979 and 1994, 97 percent of the increase went to the richest 20 percent.

In 1996, median family income increased 1.2 percent to $35,492—only the second increase since 1989. But that increase was fueled almost entirely by income gains in the South. In fact, the incomes for men with full-time jobs decreased by 0.9 percent in 1996. Many now work two and even three jobs to stay even on the wage front. And they're still paranoid about keeping their jobs and maintaining their standard of living.

SEVERAL FACTORS ARE FUELING THE JOB LOSS

Several factors are responsible for the continuing loss of jobs, despite today's robust economy. First, technological advances have allowed manufacturers to replace costly workers with computers and robots. And it's not just manufacturers replacing assembly-line workers with robots anymore. One person at a computer generating architectural drawings can replace scores of draftsmen and architects in a firm. One ATM machine can displace several bank tellers.

Hospitals, medical laboratories, libraries, purchasing departments, and personnel departments have turned to computers not only to cut costs, but to improve production and performance.

Computers, it seems, make fewer mistakes and have little or no downtime owing to illness, vacation, and family problems.

Cutthroat foreign competition is also a factor in the unprecedented job loss. Clothing, auto parts, and home furnishings are being produced more cheaply today by foreign firms using cheap labor in countries with advantageous tax laws and government support. That competition is prompting U.S. firms to take drastic measures to cut costs and remain competitive. Payroll is the first budget line to be hit.

Wall Street's eye to the bottom line and short-term shareholder profits, even at the expense of long-term health and people's jobs and lives, has also fueled the downsizing. With the Dow Jones industrial average setting record highs in the late 1990s—and corporate earnings riding high, right where shareholders want them—many see the years of corporate bloodletting as justified.

And remember, while the millions laid off from those ''disappeared'' jobs—and their families—feel the pain, and countless others experience acute job anxiety, many of those same workers make up the roughly 40 million Americans who currently own mutual funds and thereby contribute to the pressures on Wall Street for continued growth in corporate profits.

Meanwhile, the growing ease with which companies are able to outsource tasks that don't directly contribute to the bottom line has also fueled the loss of jobs. Why carry expensive jobs, with ever more costly benefits attached, if you can hire a consultant or another company to provide that service or perform that task as well, for a fixed cost that usually amounts to less?

In fact, almost 60 percent of business executives surveyed recently by Dataquest, Inc., said they now need outsourced help to offset a chronic dearth of skills.

LAYOFFS WEREN'T ALWAYS PART OF THE LANDSCAPE

So how did we get into this bind? The concept of job security ended with the age of industrialization at the turn of the century. Before the Civil War, America was an agrarian society. It took the efforts of all members of the family, even the youngest and oldest and those less able, to survive and thrive when you had to produce just about everything you consumed, wore, and used. You couldn't afford to lay off your brother, even if you wanted to. You needed that set of hands and those muscles for planting and harvest or weaving or for gathering goods from other farmers and weavers to sell in your general store.

As members of an agrarian society—as farmers or small shop-keepers or skilled craftsmen—people's lives and work were one and the same, not separate as they are today. People's homes actually were their workplaces. Work was not a distant place they traveled to, separated from the rest of their life and from their personal responsibilities. The work they performed was intertwined throughout the day and night with the other tasks of their lives. Their coworkers, or employers and employees, were their family members. People employed their family members whether they needed or wanted to precisely because they were family.

With the end of the Civil War came the Industrial Revolution and a profound change in the way people lived and worked—and in the way they thought about both. As people moved into cities and into factories, they stopped working for family and started working for a big, impersonal employer—one whose allegiance was to the stockholders and to the bottom line, not to Aunt Millie and not to you. End of job security.

No longer did a person live an integrated life where home and work were one and the same and over which he or she had relative control. With the move to the assembly line, the worker lost that integrated life, lost hours of contact each day with family, and lost control over his or her environment—especially the work environment. Work for many became a drudgery from which release came only after a seemingly endless day.

But most considered the drudgery worth it, since mass production meant affordable goods for everyone. Those who could afford little or nothing previously now could buy mass-produced clothes and appliances. With more affordable goods for all, desire for those goods grew as well. People depended on those drudgery jobs to help improve their standard of living. And with the thirst for consumer goods and services came vulnerability to the almighty employer and job insecurity. The good news was that with this mass production and new prosperity the incomes of millions of

Americans continued to grow. So while layoffs became as common as cobblestones, laid-off workers were almost guaranteed they could find a job that paid as well or better.

The Great Depression sounded a temporary sour note on this march to prosperity, but World War II changed the tune again. The United States was embarked on a race toward unprecedented economic growth, and Americans all became convinced they were entitled by birth to a piece of the American dream: a home, an automobile, a life of honest and rewarding work, and well-earned leisure and a well-heeled retirement.

While seasonal layoffs happened like clockwork in blue collar industries, most professionals and middle managers assumed when they signed on with a company at age twenty they'd still be around, albeit at a much higher corporate level, to pick up their gold watch and a healthy pension when they hit the magic retirement age forty-five years later.

But the big white collar employment boom ended in the mid-1970s and the professional and managerial job market has been percolating much more slowly ever since. To keep profits churning and to keep shareholders happy, employers have turned to the once sacrosanct ranks of professionals and middle managers for the formerly unthinkable—layoffs. That bulging budget line labeled payroll became just too enticing to ignore.

DEMOGRAPHICS

For economic reasons it's not a good time to be employed by someone else. But you're in luck. Those same economic trends indicate it's a great time to start your own freelance consulting business. Remember this: the recent Dataquest survey of business executives showed that more than 50 percent said they're now using or willing to use consultants to remain competitive. The business opportunities clearly exist for a smart, entrepreneurial professional who knows his or her business well.

That's good news. But there's other good news, in the form of demographic trends, that make this the right time to start your own freelance consulting business. That's because Americans are living longer and staying healthier than ever before. And as their lifespan lengthens many prefer to remain productive longer.

If you position yourself well, by starting your own consulting business now, at whatever age, you'll be able to continue operating that business as long as you like, and at whatever level of productivity you choose. You can decide whether you want one client or ten, whether you want to take summers off, whether you want or need $1 million in billings or $50,000, just enough to boost a pension plan or Social Security and pay for some extra luxuries.

Forget retirement, it's on the way out

For both financial and emotional reasons, the entire concept of work and retirement is changing. In fact, retirement as we now know it simply won't exist into the twenty-first century and beyond. Some simple numbers tell the story: A 1990 study by the Commonwealth Fund, a New York–based philanthropic organization, found that almost two million retired Americans ages fifty to sixty-four were interested in returning to work. According to another study, almost a third of male retirees reject retirement and return to work, mostly in the first year after they retire.

Since 1955, the American Association of Retired Persons (AARP) reports, the number of workers age forty-five and older has risen from 25 million to almost 34 million. And these older workers are no longer rushing to retire at earlier and earlier ages. From 1945 to 1982, the age at which men received their first retirement checks steadily dropped. Since 1982, however, it has remained steady at 63.7 years.

Polls by the AARP and National Council on Aging have found the closer workers get to retirement age, the more they want to continue working. Another poll found most people want to continue working after age sixty-five even if they have enough money to live well the rest of their lives. More than 90 percent say the reason is they just like working. Frankly, the thought of spending thirty years idling away their time on the links or getting a black belt in shopping or ceramics sends them into spasms of despair. So why not work for yourself and share the wisdom you've earned?

Financially, retirement may be a bust

Many people are finding they simply can't maintain the kind of lifestyle they want on their combination of Social Security benefits, pension payments, and savings. They need more money.

Perhaps, like millions of people before you, you've bought the American retirement dream as packaged by Madison Avenue for political and business convenience. That meant following a rigidly sequential path through life from nursery to school, then to work, and finally to the long-sought reward: easy retirement. But the concept of retirement isn't a natural part of the life cycle of any animal, including humans. And despite the slick propaganda we've all come to believe as gospel, it isn't a right granted every U.S. citizen at birth.

Retirement actually was created in the depths of the Great Depression by the Social Security Act of 1935, as a means of curing wholesale unemployment. It worked for a time. Forcing older workers—those over age sixty-five—to retire opened up scores of jobs for younger ones.

But financially the retirement dream isn't going to work for you as it did for your parents. The Social Security system today is ailing, if not quite expired. If inflation, increased longevity, and the wave of baby boomer retirements looming on the horizon don't kill it off, it will have to be resuscitated in a much different form. With 76 million baby boomers reaching traditional retirement age, there are more folks getting ready to cash into Social Security benefits at one time than ever before. And those already receiving benefits are living longer than previous generations. That means they'll be collecting Social Security benefits longer, too.

Private pension plans are going broke and being dismantled. People today aren't saving like their parents did so they won't have fat bank accounts to fall back on. And real estate isn't climbing in value as it once did, so they won't have big stashes of "hidden" wealth to add to their retirement riches.

Your emotions will be a factor too

Emotionally, you're going to need more than traditional retirement can offer. Through advances in medicine, nutrition, and technology, people today are healthier and living decades longer than they did sixty years ago. They don't want to stop being active and productive in the mature prime of life.

Think about it. All your life you've been a Type A personality—hyperactive, overachiever, workaholic. You've achieved financial security and career status by putting in killer days and working weekends, moving ever upward on at least one career ladder, maybe more. Just because you turn the magic age of sixty-five doesn't mean you're ready for the rocking chair. Many find they need more intellectual, emotional, and physical stimulation than they can find in a life without meaningful work. And establishing your own consulting business can offer you just the kind of excitement you need.

Research shows productivity is vital to health and happiness

Recent research has shown a definite correlation between work and good mental and physical health in older people. Older adults who continue working at jobs that aren't beyond their physical abilities stay healthier longer. And physical limitations are being stretched further than ever before. Anyone who has watched road races around the country and seen more and more men and women in their fifties, sixties, and even eighties competing in marathons can attest to that. These runners aren't supermen and wonder women, they've just stayed active and fit. And their high level of activity has promoted their enhanced level of fitness and performance.

Phyllis Moen, a professor of life course studies at Cornell University, has done extensive research on longevity, aging, and productivity. She said her research shows that

> *Social integration, defined by the number of roles occupied, promotes well-being, health and longevity. Being socially connected—whether through employment, volunteer work, religious activities or neighboring—is positively linked to mental and physical health and may well have greater impact on health than other roles.*
>
> *I see paid work and unpaid volunteer work as particularly integrative in that they provide culturally sanctioned ways of participating in the broader community as well as access*

to various components of society. To the degree that social integration promotes health and well-being, postretirement participation in paid jobs may extend the third stage of healthy aging, reducing demands on the health care system and enhancing quality of life.

Researchers at Yale University and the University of Michigan also have linked active aging and productivity. Based on a study of the productive activities of men and women aged seventy to seventy-nine, they found active aging adults do a third more housework, twice as much yard work, three times more paid work, and four times as much volunteer work compared with more sedentary aging persons.

Not only do activity and productivity promote health, research has also shown age isn't a reliable predictor of mental and physical abilities. In fact, when a correlation exists, research shows performance tends to improve with age in many areas. While some older adults may proceed more cautiously and deliberately in their actions, they often make fewer errors and have fewer job-related accidents.

While the stereotype of the befuddled, unproductive older adult still persists, it is now widely accepted that, in the absence of specific neurological diseases, simple aging usually does not cause any impairment in mental faculties until the mid-70s. And then, the only decrease in mental capacity that can be attributed directly to aging is some short-term memory loss.

But the research only backs up what you already know. You've been getting better at what you do every day you've done it. Experience does speak. It matters. So if you're a seasoned professional whose department has been excised and outsourced; or if you see the handwriting on the wall; or worse yet, if you've been booted and replaced by a less costly, less seasoned twenty-five-year-old, you know you've got invaluable knowledge and skills to offer your own future clients—and you can reap the profits.

IT'S A QUALITY OF LIFE DECISION

Regardless of whether they're twenty-four or fifty-four, laid off, worried about being laid off, or firmly planted on a solid, secure career path, professionals of both sexes are taking stock of their lives as they watch their children grow up and out—from afar. Many are opting out of the corporate rat race in favor of working for themselves, often as home-based consultants. It's often a quality of life decision, as it was for my friend Lynda Ford, whom I mentioned in Chapter 1. Ford says now, as the owner of The Ford Group, she has the best of both worlds, business and family, and she has them on her own terms. And she's making a good living at it, too.

Ford's not alone. Many professionals are no longer willing to sacrifice the present, and their family lives, for corporate life and the income that comes with it. They want to be able to spend quality time, not just dollars, on their families. The good news is they don't have to reduce their income expectations when they leave corporate life. Many freelance consultants work the same number of hours or more than they did as employees but bring home a much higher income. The key for them is that as business owners they are better able to adjust their work schedules to suit their own needs, including those of their families. You got it— quality of life.

One notable renegade from the corporate fast track who made national headlines is Brenda Barnes. The banner headline in *The Wall Street Journal* on September 24, 1997, read: "Top PepsiCo Executive Picks Family Over Job." Barnes, president and chief executive of Pepsi-Cola of North America at age forty-three, was considered one of the highest-ranking women in corporate America. Business experts had predicted that Barnes, a twenty-two-year veteran of PepsiCo, would be a sure bet to become CEO at a top-level consumer company, and PepsiCo itself had big plans for her.

Barnes said it was a difficult decision to leave the company she grew up with, a decision she had struggled with for a long time. But, she said, after years of hectic life as a corporate executive, traveling constantly, meeting through dinner and into the evenings and on weekends, missing out on her three children's birthdays and important events and even living in separate cities at times, she needed to give her family more of her time and attention. She also said it's not just a decision women executives are facing, but one that many male executives are confronting today as well.

Barnes hasn't said what she intends to do next, beyond focusing on her family. She hasn't ruled out a return at some point to corporate life, and she's promised PepsiCo first dibs if she does. Who knows, maybe she'll slip into a consulting business of her own? The point is, she and others who have been riding the corporate treadmill have decided it's the right time to jump off—for whatever reason.

Marcia Fox, forty-five, is another case. Fox started her own home-based communications business in 1994, when she decided to return to her career after seven years as a full-time mother. She said quality of life—specifically, her children—are the reason she is working at home. And while her home business doesn't give her extra hours with her children, she feels better being closer to them. It also allows her the flexibility to be there for them when they need her most.

Mary Kane Trochim runs her own freelance consulting business, based at home in Ithaca, New York, in partnership with her husband, Bill Trochim. Mary is president, chief executive officer, chief financial officer, and primary consulting partner. Bill developed the unique software program on which their business, Concept Systems Inc., is based. They started the business in 1994, Mary said, to do group decision-making, strategic planning, and organizational improvement projects for clients of all kinds and sizes.

"We have what we believe is a unique approach to a universal organizational problem, and want to find ways to make it easy, affordable and effective for companies and groups to do their own planning and organizational improvement," she said.

It's been exhilarating, but not easy. And while she has no regrets about switching from employee to self-employed, Mary does have some concerns. Mostly they center around concerns shared by many: money and time.

"Although we are holding our own, our bootstrap start-up has made it difficult to capitalize necessary staff expansion, market collateral development, and other operational areas that would make us work better, faster, and smarter right now," she said. "And since Bill and I are also married, our relationship sometimes—temporarily, I hope—feels like one gigantic strategic planning session for the company. I do believe we're learning, though, not to get swallowed up by it.''

Mary also noted she doesn't have the time she would like to enjoy her daughter, her home, and her ''extracurricular'' activities like dance and theater performance.

''Sometimes it's hard to tell whether the light at the end of the tunnel is the sun, or an oncoming train,'' she said.

On the other hand, she proudly pointed out, Concept Systems doubled its revenue this year and is poised for even greater growth through more targeted marketing. ''With partners we are nurturing now, our ability to consult more effectively and more knowledgeably in the areas of health service management and delivery, financial services, and telecommunications will be exponential,'' she said.

SO, THE TIME IS RIGHT

For Mary and Bill Trochim the time is clearly right. But what about you? Why not do more of what you do best, for more money, and do it for yourself?

According to a survey by the American Management Association, almost 56.7 percent of respondents said they spent more on consultants in 1994 than they did the previous year, and more than two-thirds said their spending levels would remain the same or increase in 1995. Experts say those numbers could double by the end of the century.

The biggest consulting specialties, according to the survey, are information technology, 69 percent; training, 63 percent; and strategic planning, 40 percent. But with the level of outsourcing happening today, there are plenty of opportunities for accomplished professionals in a variety of fields. Remember, a consultant is someone who is paid to give advice to someone else. You don't have to be an expert in every field, but you do have to know how to find the information or skills your client needs. If you're experienced, with a good track record you can point to; if you're creative and resourceful; if you're good with people and are willing and able to sell yourself, now is the time to put those strengths to work for yourself.

WHAT ABOUT MONICA DUBOIS
AND AARON STEINBERG?

Monica and Aaron took different routes to reach the same conclusion—that the time was right to start their own consulting businesses. For Monica the path was a very painful one on a very personal level. She experienced her first real failure, and then made a very costly false start.

Aaron didn't face immediate personal failure, but he watched his friends disappearing from the work world around him, and he felt great sympathy for their plight. But Aaron didn't let those ominous signs unsettle him. Instead, he looked beyond the immediate empty desks and saw what those desks meant to his company and others. Some of those gaps were being filled in-house, no question about it. But he also was astute enough to pick up on another trend—outsourcing. He read enough to know that many companies were seeking outside help, through consultants or subcontractors, to fill the gaps.

That's when he decided to turn that trend into the opportunity he'd been waiting for—and preparing for—all his life. Aaron Steinberg wanted desperately to be an entrepreneur, and he saw that the economic trends that were cold, harsh reality for so many could provide him with the opportunity he needed.

WHAT NEXT?

As you've just learned, the time couldn't be more advantageous for a freelance consultant—both from an economic sense and a demographic sense. So, if you've made the decision to start your own freelance consulting business, it's time to get down to business and do the homework you need to get done to get your business off the ground. Your homework assignments start in Chapter 3, so sharpen your pencils and read on.

3

DO YOUR HOMEWORK

Some might say the hardest part is behind you. The soul-searching, gut-wrenching, night-sweating, tea leaf–reading, decision-making process is over. The decision's made. At least for now. You've decided you've got what it takes to be a successful entrepreneur, and the time is right for leaving the corporate world to launch your own enterprise. Now it's time to get down to the business of starting your own business. While that might sound overwhelming at first, not to worry. That's why you bought this book, remember?

Starting a business can be almost as simple as baking a cake. Just follow the instructions. I'll outline in the chapters to come step by step, and you can't miss. So grab your business notebook and pencil and let's get started. Much of what we'll be doing in this chapter will be research designed to help you figure out exactly what form your business should take, who your clients and market should be, and what your competition is doing—so you can do it better. It's basic homework that will provide another reality check on whether you're headed in the right direction in starting your own freelance consulting business. A safety check, in fact, that will help you determine whether you are positioning yourself and your business to ensure maximum success.

HOW MUCH CAN YOU EARN?

The first piece of homework you'll want to attend to before diving too deeply into your research is to calculate a rough estimate of how much you can reasonably expect to earn as a business consultant. This will be important down the road in helping you to structure your financing, your business plan, and your expectations for the next year or two. While your earnings and profit will depend on your skills, personality, and drive, as well as the market and the competition, there are some basic guidelines from which you can make calculations.

For example, the average new business consulting service operated by the owner without employees, can sell between $75,000 and $125,000 in business in a year—not the first year, usually, but often by year two. That assumes you're earning from $75 to $125 an hour, four hours a day, five days a week. The other four and more hours a day you'll be doing administrative paperwork, marketing, and networking.

You can calculate your profit from those earnings. First, determine the bare minimum you need to live on. Say, $25,000. That will be your "salary" for your first two years. That labor cost will be your biggest expense, as it is in any business.

You can expect overhead expenses, such as rent, equipment, telephone, and advertising to total 25 percent of your presalary earnings, while direct expenses, such as stationery, subscriptions, books, and client entertainment will total 10 percent. Those expenses total 35 percent of your revenue.

If you earn $80,000 the second year, those expenses add up to approximately $28,000. If you add in your salary of $25,000, your expenses total $53,000. So you can figure your profit from there. Don't forget taxes, though. It's only net profit after you subtract taxes. In year two, if your earnings total $80,000 and you rent work space, your net profit before taxes will be $27,000.

If you eliminate the rent expense by working at home, you can cut overhead to 15 percent and increase your profit. So, if you earned $80,000 your second year and work out of your home, your net profit before taxes will be roughly $35,000.

Don't expect such riches your first year, when you're still trying to find client one or two and are buying equipment and supplies. During your first year you can probably expect to bring in just 75 percent of that second-year revenue, or, for example, $56,250. Overhead that first year could be as high as 40 percent, or $22,500; labor, 40 percent, $22,500; direct expenses, 10 percent, $5,625.

That leaves just $5,625 before-tax profit. Some suggest 70 percent of your first-year expense budget should go toward marketing. If you follow that advice you can kiss any profit goodbye the first year. So before starting out, be sure you can live on your salary and be sure you have a healthy cushion to fall back on if clients come more slowly than you expect.

MAKING THE TRANSITION

If you've been downsized out of a job, chances are good you've been handed a severance package you can use to finance the establishment of your new business or use as a safety net. If you're still employed but see the handwriting on the wall, or simply have concluded you want to work for yourself, there are several ways to ensure you make a smooth and secure transition from employee to self-employed management consultant.

Change your attitude about work

Remember, as a corporate employee you can't count on a gold watch for longevity any longer, and the words _job security_ have flown out the window. The psychology of the workplace has changed forever, and in order to be successful in the twenty-first century and beyond—and ensure a smooth transition from being an employee to self-employment—you need to alter the way you think about work and career.

Stephen Pollan and Mark Levine, in their best-selling book _Die Broke_ (HarperCollins, 1997) said in order to live successfully in the "new world" you have to learn four new, simple maxims: "quit today, pay cash, don't retire and die broke."

The psychology behind the first, "quit today," is worth reviewing here. Pollan and Levine suggest that for too long, our national work ethic and culture have encouraged people to identify themselves and their status with their jobs. And, they say, when you live in a world where there's no such thing as corporate loyalty, it's dangerous both psychologically and financially to think of yourself and your job as one.

They say the answer is to "mentally separate yourself from your employer and realize that you're on your own."

The same advice is true for you. It's important now, as you actually separate yourself physically from your employer, to do so mentally as well. No one's going to look out for you any longer except you—but then, as Pollan and Levine point out, no one else has been doing that anyway—certainly not your employer.

They go further, suggesting you "instead adopt a mercantile approach: focus on what you're doing as a job—that word your grandmother used—not necessarily a career, and view your job as primarily an income-generating device; any other benefits are purely secondary. Having a mercantile approach doesn't mean obsessing over money. It simply means using your job to generate the money you need to pursue your personal goals, rather than looking to the job itself to fulfill these goals."

The key in making your transition is attitude. Separate yourself from the employee frame of mind. You're on your own, and need to take care of business yourself. Don't get overcome with the vision of this new business as an all-consuming, end-in-itself career. Forget the word *career*. It's just a job, a means to an end. And the end is the good life. The job—even when it's your own consulting business—doesn't define who or what you are, but simply allows you to be. In that way it can be constantly evolving to meet both your needs and that of the marketplace.

Those thoughts should take a world of stress and strain off your shoulders and help you get on with the job at hand: transitioning into your new business.

Try moonlighting first

One way to ensure a smooth transition is to moonlight for a while. That's right, start your new management consulting business while still employed full time. Moonlighting is nothing new, and in fact is quite common. A recent survey by the Independent Insurance Agents of America found that 59 percent of home-based business owners operate less than forty hours a week, while only 40 percent of home businesses run full time—more than forty hours a week.

And those part-time businesses generated almost $11 million in income.

There are several advantages to moonlighting as you start your new business. First, it provides a financial cushion. You also can take your time and start slowly, finding new clients and the right business format while still paying the bills with you regular salary. Moonlighting also provides a fertile field for finding clients for your new business—you can network and line up clients and contacts from your current job. These are people you've already worked with, so they know exactly what they can expect from you in terms of performance. That's a big plus for a new entrepreneur.

One downside to moonlighting is the stress and energy involved in trying to perform two jobs well simultaneously. Another is that you have to squeeze your new clients, those you're trying to woo, into after hours and weekends. Many are accommodating, but others simply don't want the hassle. You may end up skipping lunches for a while, as you try to juggle both jobs.

While most moonlighting entrepreneurs keep their new businesses secret from their employers, that's not always necessary. In fact, both employer and employee can benefit from the arrangement. Sam Seigleman started his training consultancy while still working as training director at a California media company. He didn't have the resources to go out on his own at the start, so he continued working at his day job while networking and lining up projects for his own clients.

Then, when he felt he was almost ready to strike out on his own, he told his employer about his new business. His employer asked him to stay on for four months to help with the transition, and he agreed. During that time he spent two-thirds of his workday on his employer's business and a third on his own. That allowed him to get his business more firmly established before he released his safety net, but it also gave his employer the time needed to find and train his replacement. In addition, his employer was smart enough to realize that in Seigleman he had a reenergized employee with fresh enthusiasm and ideas, including those he was picking up from his new clients.

Mark Santoro used a different approach. He started his organizational development consultancy while still employed but quickly realized his long daily commute would make it almost impossible to do justice to both his day job and to developing his new business. So he told his employer about his business plans and arranged to continue working at his job three days a week (at three-fifths his former pay) while working for himself the other two-plus days. Again, the arrangement proved beneficial for both parties and allowed Santoro to get his business firmly grounded before cutting loose from his job. Better yet, he left the company with an added bonus—his former boss became one of his first contract clients.

OPPORTUNITY KNOCKS ON MANY DOORS

Whether you decide to transition slowly into your new business or go cold turkey, you need to know exactly what business you're embarking on before you make a move. And there's a world of opportunity out there. Businesses today need and purchase advice from consultants in almost every field, including:

☛ FINANCES

accounting	investments
budget	insurance
banking	real estate
acquisitions	pensions

☛ HUMAN RESOURCES

benefits	management
personnel	travel
training	records management
executive search	recreation

☛ COMMUNICATIONS

advertising
marketing
public relations
publications

government, community
   affairs
printing and graphics

☛ RESEARCH AND DEVELOPMENT

economics
engineering
import/export
international business

telecommunications
entrepreneurship
strategic planning

☛ OPERATIONS

quality control
sales
data processing
construction

production
packaging
information systems

Opportunities exist in all of these areas. What you need to do next is figure out exactly what you can offer clients.

Traits every management consultant needs

Successful management consultants share some key skills. From a study of twenty-five well-established, independent national consultants—reported by Nancy Veazey and Virginia Bianco-Mathis in the July 1996 *Training & Development*—four key skills were identified: "listening, marketing through continuous networking, authenticity and assertiveness in addressing interpersonal issues, and intuition."

Veazey and Bianco-Mathis further concluded that successful

consultants need to live "an examined life," are "driven by the need to make a difference through helping others," and are "equally dedicated to both the process and outcomes."

Successful consultants also are problem solvers. You need to be able to identify and analyze the problem; devise a solution; implement the solution; then evaluate its effectiveness and determine whether modifications are needed. That's the basic process you follow.

But while those general skills are important for overall success, in order to establish your consulting business you need to define exactly what specific skills you have and what services you and you alone can offer clients. What, exactly, do they need done that you can do for them?

Keep in mind that most management consultants provide either a specific service—for example, provide training to managers in strategic planning—or solve problems, or both. If a company's sales have been flat for several years you might be asked to figure out what's wrong and advise the firm on how to fix it. If you don't have the right set of skills to undertake both parts of that assignment you can subcontract out the part you can't handle, such as sales force retraining. The important thing is to know exactly what business you're in, what services you can provide clients, and then stick to what you can do well. That's the way to keep clients coming back and spreading the good word.

DEFINE YOUR NEW BUSINESS

First, you have to define what you can do for clients. So, right now, get out your business notebook and make several lists: first, list all the special training and education you've had—in school, in the workplace, and anyplace else you can think of. Next, list your specific skills. If your field is communications, for example, can you write press releases, edit, handle media placements and relations, do desktop publishing, write advertising copy, produce brochures, do public relations, strengthen community and government relations—or all of the above?

As you evaluate and list your specific skills, areas of expertise, and experience you will begin to define your business—what it is you can do for clients. You also need to consider what potential clients might need. You can specialize in several kinds of related tasks, but if your focus is too broad you'll lose the edge specialization brings.

Now, ask yourself the following questions and write the answers in your notebook.

What kinds of business experience do I have?

What specific skills and accomplishments can I point to?

What training, formal and informal, have I completed?

What knowledge and skills will I need to become an effective consultant in the areas I'm considering?

What do I enjoy doing for others?

Do I prefer working directly or indirectly with others?

What are my main interests and hobbies?

Do many consultants offer these services in this region?

Am I willing to seek and service clients beyond the region, electronically and through travel?

Carefully review your answers to the questions above. They'll help you determine what consulting services you're best suited to offer and whether there's a potential market for those services.

Now, think in terms of the brochure you'll soon be preparing to help you market your business. To help you further define your business, visualize what specific tasks you will offer clients in that brochure. For example, in her brochure, Lynda Ford tells potential clients she provides human resource–related services in the areas of compensation and salary administration, benefits administration, workers' compensation and safety, recruiting, total quality management, training and development, and special projects. Under each of those headings she lists specific tasks.

For example, under compensation and salary administration she lists: compensation system evaluation, job evaluations and descriptions, salary range analysis and calculation, and performance appraisals.

Do one more exercise to help you crystallize, in your own mind, exactly what your business will be. It's called the "elevator exercise.'' Pretend you've landed in an elevator with your dream potential client and you've got three floors to go before you both get out. How would you pitch your business to this potential client in this time? One or two sentences is all you'll be able to get in, so make them count.

For example, ''We specialize in developing and implementing marketing and promotion campaigns for new businesses.'' Or, ''We provide a full range of human resource services, acting as human resource director, for small companies.''

That should help you begin to sketch the outlines of your consulting business. Now you need to define your target market. That will tell you whether you can expect your future business to succeed, or whether you need to go back to the drawing board and further sharpen your focus. This market analysis will also help you later when you map out your business and marketing plans.

Define your target market

First, define your ideal client. You need to figure out exactly who would be most interested in contracting for your services. Then decide whether there are enough of those clients within your reach—whether that be close to home or around the globe—to support your business.

Just remember, although your business will be based at home and a lot of consulting work is information based and can be handled electronically, most clients still won't hire people to perform an important task without spending time with them in person. They also want to be sure you have a feel for their business. So while in theory the whole world can be your target market, be sure you understand and accept that in reality, at least at the start, you'll need to aim closer to home.

You'll also need to pinpoint where and how you can reach potential clients, because your future marketing will be targeted to where those clients can be found.

Now, close your eyes and envision your future clients. List everything you can find out about them. If you're going to provide a full range of human resource services for small- to mid-size companies, try to establish a portrait of both the businesses that might need your services and the people who run those businesses. Are the businesses new or ones looking for a turnaround? Perhaps they're those struggling to join the technological age. Perhaps any business within a certain size range is fair game.

What are their owners' characteristics? Are they male or female, young, middle-aged, or older CEOs at the peak of their business careers? What's their income, where do they live, where do they shop and what are their hobbies? Contact relevant industry or trade groups relating to your target clients for possible demographic information.

Depending on what your consulting specialty is, your clients can be just about anyone. The possibilities are endless, and it'll be up to you to decide exactly who you want to target specifically and go after them.

Let's say you're going to specialize in formulating and implementing strategic plans. Every business, large and small—but particularly stale ones—can get a jump start from an effective strategic plan. To start out, you may want to look at small- to moderate-size local and regional businesses that appear moderately but not hugely successful and that haven't changed much in recent years. Look for signs that the businesses could use a makeover, then target the owners. Create a detailed portrait of these businesses and their owners.

The shotgun strategy will land some clients, but a more targeted, focused approach will continue to reap rewards when the shotgun runs out of ammunition.

Keep in mind this advice from Mary Kane Trochim, co-owner with her husband, Bill, of the consulting firm Concept Systems, Inc.:

I sense that companies and institutions who routinely employ the larger consulting corporations, mostly for 'insurance' purposes, are going to be more inclined to do their homework and find consulting companies much more specifically targeted to the client's needs, and much more flexible and easy to manage. The unbelievable explosion in consulting as a profession over the last ten years is marked by agility, subject matter expertise coupled with consulting skill in very targeted areas or markets, and a great deal of savvy on the part of the client, who now knows what to ask of their consultant candidates in advance of developing the interminable dependency relationship that has been the hallmark of big-gun consulting for so long.

Relationship is at the heart of consulting agreements these days, but companies are increasingly relying upon their own internal capabilities, enhanced by, but not turned over to, the external consulting companies. Companies are seeking real value, real results upon which the next improvement need can be built, rather than addressing company concerns by calling in advisers to work on isolated issues. Opportunities abound for consultants who are well-informed, diligent, and client focused, provided they also have and bring to their jobs a real distinction—with a difference—that sets them apart from the average individual consultant.

Analyze the market potential

Now that you know who your target clients are, you need to decide how big the potential market for your services is and where future clients can be found. Chances are your market, at least initially, will be your local and regional community. Depending on the nature of your consulting business, you'll need to ask yourself some of the following questions:

Do you live in a thriving community with a sufficient number of small- and moderate-size businesses?

Is your downtown business section vital?

Is there a thriving business and technology park?

Are there good opportunities for young professionals or new service businesses?

Are there colleges or technical schools with enthusiastic graduates?

Are more people moving into the area than are moving out?

Or, should you market your consulting services to a wider market via the Internet or through national business publications?

As a business consultant specializing in strategic planning you'll need to target business owners, and you'll find them at Rotary and Kiwanis, the downtown businessperson's association, and the Chamber of Commerce. Or they'll be keeping in shape while making their own contacts at health clubs and on golf courses or relaxing at the symphony.

Check the Yellow Pages and the business sections of local newspapers and magazines for news about start-ups, especially those with five to seventy-five employees. Contact the Chamber of Commerce to get a complete listing of small- to mid-size businesses in your region. Look at those within a two- to three-hour drive from your home. Make lists of potential clients. Before making sales calls, you'll need to research the individual companies on your target list.

Later, when we talk more about a specific marketing plan, we'll take the carefully defined portrait of your clients we settled on earlier and decide exactly where they can be found. That's where you'll target your future marketing. But for now, you just need to determine that there are sufficient potential clients within reach who would be willing and able to purchase your service.

Check out the competition

You need to touch base with others in the field, but this can be problematic. Obviously, a potential competitor isn't going to be eager to share much useful information. So you have to assure the consultants you contact that you'll be specializing in services quite different from theirs and therefore won't be a competitor. Find out how they got started, how they advertise and market themselves, what they would do differently if they were starting out today. Ask about their successes and their failures, their client likes and dislikes, their do's and don'ts. You'd be surprised at how willing business owners are to talk about their businesses if they can feel assured you won't be trying to steal their clients.

You might also suggest your partnering with them in the future if you can offer skills they often need and vice versa. Such project-by-project partnerings contractually or subcontractually are becoming much more common, as consultants realize they need to improve their mix of skills in order to appeal to a broader market. So keep networking and partnering in mind as you check out the competition.

You also might consider hiring your own consultant, both to see how he or she operates his or her own business and for genuine help getting started. Rhonda Abrams, a small business consultant who writes a syndicated newspaper column, just celebrated her tenth year as a consulting entrepreneur. When she was starting out, she said, she hired an established consultant to help her narrow her focus and find her own consulting niche.

Discuss your plan with potential clients

You also need to test your idea with potential clients. Check with friends and neighbors who are business executives on their need for your service.

You need to ask potential clients, what are their goals and key priorities in their purchase of your service? Why do they want or need this service? Do they want you to solve their problems or teach them how to solve their own problems? How much are they willing to pay for this service? How often would they use it?

Then, conduct an informal survey of potential clients you don't know or don't normally come in contact with. Try random cold-calling on the telephone, but be ready for the cold shoulder or worse, the sound of the phone slamming in your ear. Many business people don't like to be bothered, but it's certainly worth the effort for what might be a valuable insight from those more objective than your friends and family. Work your way down the list of target businesses you compiled earlier.

You also can bounce your idea off an independent observer by contacting the local office of the Small Business Administration. The SBA sponsors a mentor program called SCORE (Service Corps of Retired Executives), which brings together retired executives and people who are trying to launch a business. Their advice is free, impartial, and rooted in experience.

Turn yourself into an expert

You'll need to "credentialize" yourself as an expert in your field. Your previous experience as an employee will be helpful in this, particularly if you can point to specific projects you led or get testimonials from previous clients or coworkers. You also can establish yourself as an expert by writing articles and books and making speeches at seminars, conventions, and local business groups. Then you network. And not just by joining the Kiwanis or Rotary and handing out your business card. You need to create an image of yourself as a respected leader in the field, so that when there's a need for someone who does what you do, your name will roll off businesspeople's tongues.

HERE'S WHAT MONICA DID

Monica was lucky that she hadn't gotten as far as selling her home in a small Northeastern city and moving her family to Washington, D.C., where corporate headquarters was located. When she was fired she returned home, and once she got the disastrous mailing and packaging business out of her system she was able to tap into her old network of friends and business associates to look for clients for her consulting business.

Unfortunately, that's what she did first, look for clients. She put a series of ads in the local paper and printed up a business card that she posted around town and dropped off at small- and moderate-size businesses in a 50-mile radius of her home. The problem is, she hadn't figured out exactly what her business mission and objectives would be, what services she wanted to offer clients, or where and how she would set up her office. She hadn't even decided how much to charge for her services.

Monica's first client came from her networking efforts. When she returned to town she rejoined the board of directors of the local United Way, and the first client was another board member, the owner of a small printing company. Monica got the job because she knew her business, not because of any persuasive business brochures or testimonials—which she didn't have. She also got the job because she underpriced her services—she decided to ask for just $65 an hour—and the business owner, who'd been shopping around, knew a good deal when he saw it.

Monica hadn't bothered to check out her competition's fees, hadn't looked at her expenses, and hadn't figured out how much business she needed to bring in to earn the income she needed. But, she had her first client, did a good job on what admittedly was a quickie, month-long assignment, and signed him on for another, longer-term, project.

By that time she'd checked around a bit and done some calculating, and realized she had to get her financial act together if she was going to make it as a business owner. She raised her fee to $90 an hour—an increase that kept her a bit under the competition but in the ballpark, and which she justified by the increased complexity of the assignment and additional services she would provide.

Monica wasn't there yet, but she was learning, by the seat of her pants and by trial and error. That can be costly, but it's one way to learn.

AARON DID THINGS DIFFERENTLY, AGAIN

Aaron's a list maker. Before he ever printed up his business card he made lists of the services he thought he might offer, lists of the businesses he thought might find those services useful, lists of the characteristics of the kinds of people who run those businesses, lists of the kinds of places he might find those people, lists of the kinds of organizations and activities he should begin to participate in to extend his network of potential contacts and clients—and on and on.

Aaron filled a notebook with his lists and calculations. He calculated how much he needed to earn, calculated what his expenses would be in his first solo year, looked into what his competitors were charging and how they were marketing and advertising themselves, and kept building up his special fund.

He also decided to focus his business on a specific niche that he felt was up for grabs and offered a wealth of opportunity: established businesses that needed a fresh, new image, and a fresh, new public relations and marketing campaign to spur sales. Aaron decided he would help these businesses transform themselves for business in the twenty-first century and beyond. The concept excited his creative instincts, and he thought he could use it to help excite the creative, competitive instincts of prospective clients. Aaron had carefully defined his market.

NOW, WHAT ABOUT YOU?

Okay, you're an expert, and you've done the homework outlined in this chapter. You've determined your financial needs and determined there's a market for your services. There's still a lot of basic groundwork to be done before you sign on your first client. In Chapter 4 we'll get down to the basics of mapping out your business and marketing plans. With those you'll be well on the road to starting your new consulting business.

4

GET DOWN TO BUSINESS

You've determined exactly what services your consulting firm will offer, and have confirmed there's a market for those services. Now you need to draw up a business plan and a separate marketing plan to provide you with a road map in starting your business. Sound, detailed planning is the key to success for every entrepreneur, including the owner of a consulting service.

Just as you wouldn't dream of beginning a long journey to an unknown destination without a map, you shouldn't consider starting your consulting business without a business plan and a marketing plan. They will help you map out the route you'll follow to meet your business goals. You'll also be able to check your progress regularly against your plans, and fine-tune them as your own experience and market conditions suggest.

But before you tackle your business plan, what you need to do now is nail down the legal form your business will take.

As a freelance consultant just starting out, chances are you'll want to form a sole proprietorship. That means you own the business alone, are entitled to all its profits, and are responsible for all its debts. A sole proprietorship provides you with maximum control of the business and minimum government interference. It's the legal form used by more than 75 percent of all businesses.

There are several advantages to forming a sole partnership: the ease with which it can be started, the freedom you have to make all business decisions, and that all the profits are yours and yours alone. Except for what you owe Uncle Sam in taxes, of course.

It does have some disadvantages, though: you are liable for all business debts. And if those should exceed your business assets, your personal assets are at risk as well. Sole proprietorships also have more difficulty raising capital, should that be necessary. Still, as an independent consultant a sole proprietorship should suit you well in the beginning.

Other options are a partnership or incorporation. A partnership is a consulting business owned by two or more people who agree to share the profits. A corporation is different from the other legal forms of business because it is considered legally to be an artificial entity with the same rights and responsibilities as a human being. Unlike a sole proprietorship, it has an existence separate from its owners. Other options include subchapter S corporations and limited liability companies.

Those other forms have their own advantages and disadvantages, and you should discuss them with your accountant and attorney. The advantages primarily are decreased personal liability. The disadvantages generally are higher taxes and costs. For most freelance consultants, a sole proprietorship is the way to go . . . at first. With that settled, we need to deal with some nuts and bolts financial issues.

HOW MUCH SHOULD YOU CHARGE?

Deciding what to charge for your services is not as easy as you might expect. Sure, most management consulting fees fall within a general range: between $55 and $150 an hour, or from $250 to $10,000 a day, with a median daily rate of $3,000. You could just pick a magic number.

But it's important for you to look at several factors carefully before setting your fee schedule. Those factors include your costs, the number of billable hours you can devote to clients, the competition, and less measurable but equally important, the value you place on your services. Remember, as much as 50 percent of your working time won't be billable hours because they'll be devoted to marketing, networking, and administrative work, so your fee structure will have to cover that time as well.

A quick mathematical formula can give you a rough idea of what you need to charge. Here's how it works: First, take the total number of paid hours you plan to work (let's assume for now the clients are there) during the next year, excluding vacation, seminars, and nonbillable hours. Next estimate how much money you'll need for the year, excluding whatever expenses you can bill directly to clients. Then divide the first number into the second to come up with the hourly rate you need to charge.

Say you plan to work five days a week, eight full working hours a day. But 50 percent of those hours will be nonbillable, so drop the number down to 20 hours a week. Take two weeks off for vacation and another week for a seminar or training session. That's 49 weeks times 20 hours, or 980 paid hours. Say you estimate you need $100,000 a year to cover your overhead, marketing, and living expenses, including vacation and kids' camps, mortgage, etc. Divide 980 into 100,000 and you get an hourly rate of $102. That's a start.

But what if your estimate of billable hours is off? What if, for example, you don't get the steady stream of clients you anticipate, or have to turn a few down because they all come at once? Or what if your competition is charging $75 an hour or $200? One thing to keep in mind is that American consumers have bought into the concept of paying for quality. U.S. businesspeople, by and large, believe they are getting better value, or better advice, if they have to pay more for it. Not exorbitantly more, but more. And they tend to heed that advice more reliably.

So be sure to tack a "value" tax onto your fee. And don't stray too drastically from what the competition is charging. If you're way under-priced, prospective clients will assume you're not very good at what you do. If you're way over-priced relative to the competition, prospective clients will want to know why, and if you don't have a good reason they'll assume you don't know very much about the market and don't have good business sense.

You can also take a different approach in pricing, rather than the hourly rate formula. You can adopt a more direct approach to selling value by pricing based on results instead of time. For example, if you're a sales consultant you can charge a percentage of increase in sales. If you're a human resources consultant you can charge a percentage of the client's total human resources budget.

This way, you avoid the too-easy, not-always-accurate comparisons with competitors' price lists.

Lynda Ford bases her fees on a combination of both an hourly rate and a project model. She set her general hourly rate based on the going rates for consultants in her market, which she knows is less than the hourly rate in more metropolitan markets. Then she analyzes the project, estimates the amount of time it will take, and multiplies by her hourly rate, factors in any special needs or materials, and comes up with a project fee. And now that she's branching into bigger markets via the Internet, she's adjusting her hourly rate to reflect the competition in those markets.

Finally, don't forget to charge back to your client any expenses you incur as a direct result of an assignment. You'll want to be sure your client understands in advance that he or she will be billed for these expenses, which can include such items as:

Travel expenses, including airline or train tickets, and mileage

Overnight mail charges

Telephone calls

Hotel and meal costs while on assignment

Materials for special items

Books and special software

Now that you've a good idea of what you'll charge your clients, you're almost ready to draft your business plan. But first you need to enlist a team of professionals with whom you will work in the coming years to protect and nurture your business. You won't be employing such professionals on staff, but you'll need their services nonetheless, and the sooner you bring them on board the better off you'll be. Their advice will prove well worth the cost in the years to come.

Put together your own team

This team of professionals will help guide you through the process of starting your consulting business. You'll need an accountant and a banker. You'll also need a lawyer to prepare any contracts you may enter into with clients and to research any licenses and permits you may need. If you don't have such professionals lined up, do it now.

As an experienced professional who already has established a career, you may not have to go far to find skilled, responsible help. Consider those you know well from your past career and whose skills you have come to respect, or ask other consultants for suggestions.

Don't make the classic mistake of hiring someone just to be a nice guy, or to fulfill a family or friendship obligation. This should be a business decision like any other, and you need the wisdom and experience of seasoned, successful professionals as you start your own business. Speaking of seasoned, don't overlook the cadre of experienced semi-retirees with part-time businesses.

Check with the SBA's mentor program, SCORE, which I mentioned in the preceding chapter. Also check with the American Association of Retired Persons (AARP), with professional associations, and with friends and associates in other businesses for candidates. Ask candidates for a free initial meeting and if they decline, cross them off your list. Ask for the names of three recent clients. Contact these references and ask their opinion of the candidate's professional skills and services.

These are key decisions and you need to make them carefully and thoughtfully. Your team will help guide your future, so check their credentials, their references, and their business premises carefully. Call the Better Business Bureau and the state Division of Consumer Affairs before you sign them up to represent you in your new business.

DRAFT YOUR BUSINESS PLAN

Your business plan will be an important part of your business notebook and your future. It will serve as your road map to success as it guides every step of your business planning and operation. While it will be detailed, it need not be elaborate, since you won't be submitting it to a commercial lender in hopes of obtaining a business loan. (More about that later, but generally, commercial lenders do not finance small business start-ups. If you need financing, you'll get it elsewhere.)

The plan should address your business's mission, your goals and objectives, and your strategy and finances. In other words, it should summarize your business goals, the strategy you will use to reach those goals, and the resources you will need. Preparation of your business plan is not something you do as an intellectual exercise and then stick in a drawer and forget about, or something you do to impress someone else. It should be both real and realistic, and something you refer to every day as you make decisions about the operation of your business. It should be, more than anything, a useful tool.

Below I'll give you a general outline you can follow in drafting your business plan, as well as a sample plan for a fictional consulting business. But before drafting your business plan you need to touch base with others in the field. We talked about this a bit in Chapter 3, when you were analyzing your target market. But you need to run this drill again now, before drafting your business plan. And perhaps yet again later, when you draft your complete marketing plan.

As I said earlier, it can be problematic, so you have to assure the consultants you contact that you'll be specializing in services quite different from theirs and therefore won't be a competitor. Obviously, a potential competitor isn't going to be eager to help you find a way to steal his business.

Find out how they got started, who their clients are and how they found them, how they advertise and market themselves, and what they would do differently if they were starting out today. Ask about their successes and their failures, their client likes and dislikes, and their do's and don'ts. Business owners usually are happy to talk about their businesses if they feel assured you won't be trying to steal their clients.

Consider this advice from Lynda Ford: ''The best advice I could probably give to somebody considering becoming an independent consultant is to pick as many people's brains as you can before getting into this.''

Ford said before she even started on her business plan she called the New York State–run Small Business Development Center, which gave her great free information and materials. In addition, she met with two members of SCORE.

Ford said she hoped the SCORE volunteers would give her advice on preparing her business plan. Instead, she said, they made her do most of the talking. "I thought, that's not what I wanted, I wanted them to do the talking." But, she added, by the end of the session she realized exactly how smart they had been. "Instead of just telling me what to do, they made me think through exactly what I wanted to do and how I should do it. They helped me to crystallize my ideas."

Ford also suggested setting up your own informal board of directors. Call on people whose opinion you trust, people in the business community you admire. Ask them for advice, run your ideas by them and pick their brains. Ford called her lawyer and her accountant, a woman in the community she admires who has her own successful business and another, older male consultant who ended up giving her his client list—he'd decided he was ready to retire.

You'll find that most successful businesspeople are eager to share their war stories and even some secrets, provided you won't be a direct competitor. In fact, when it comes to talking about their businesses, it's often hard to get enthusiastic entrepreneurs to stop.

One other observation Ford made about her conversations with SCORE and with local business owners: "It really gives you an appreciation of the business community in your area."

Call potential clients again

You also need to fine-tune your concept with potential clients before drafting your plan. Get out your list of target clients and call some of them again. Ask them to assess their need for and interest in the list of services you intend to provide. What are their goals and key priorities? Would the services you intend to provide help them achieve those goals? Why do they want or need this service? Do they want you to solve their problems or teach them how to solve their own problems? How much are they willing to pay for this service? How often would they use it?

Their responses will help you fine-tune your plan and keep your expectations realistic. If you base your business plan on pie-in-the-sky expectations and goals, you'll not only get off to a bad start, you may cross the finish line before you even have a chance to hit your stride.

Here's a general guide for a business plan

Now you're ready to tackle your business plan. Here's a general outline you can follow:

General information. List the name of your business, your name and address, telephone, fax, and E-mail numbers.

Mission statement. This should be a general statement of one or two sentences explaining your overall goal in starting this business and exactly what services you provide for clients.

Objectives. List your specific goals and objectives for the business.

Define the business. Describe the business: What consulting services will you provide and to whom; how will you provide those services; where and how will you reach your clients; who's your primary competition; will you need to hire employees?

Rate structure. Include both basis (hourly, daily, project) and rates for specific services.

Finances. We'll discuss finances in more detail later in this chapter, but include realistic income and expense projections. Allow some cushion for unexpected start-up costs and setbacks, and for slower-than-expected growth. Remember, it will take time for people to get to know you and your business, and to get into the habit of calling on you.

Here's an example of a business plan, including a first-year financial plan, you can use as a guide:

SAMPLE BUSINESS PLAN

General information

The Powers Agency
378 Fulton Place
Ithaca, NY 14850
607-337-6215
Fax 607-338-3451
E-mail: jkp12@aol.com

Mission statement

The Powers Agency will provide market research and newspaper editorial and design services to community newspapers with circulations of 5,000 to 15,000 that are seeking to attract new readers and advertisers.

The business

The Powers Agency will be owned and operated initially as a one-person, home-based business from the home of president and consultant Jacqueline K. Powers, at 378 Fulton Place in Ithaca, NY 14850. She will subcontract work on projects as needed.

Ms. Powers is seeking to borrow $8,000 to finance the start-up of the business, including an upgraded computer and information system for her home office, and for marketing and promotion. She will use $10,000 of her own money for additional start-up and first-year operating expenses and for living expenses.

The market

The business is aimed at small newspapers that have been experiencing flat or decreasing advertising and circulation growth. Its purpose is to provide these newspapers, located mainly in nonmetropolitan areas, with design and editorial services, tailored to research in their market, that will produce a revitalized newspaper with a wider advertising base and increased circulation.

The business initially will cater to family-owned newspapers and those owned by smaller, privately-owned groups on the East Coast. Initial clients will be a chain of small weeklies in the Tompkins County area in which Ms. Powers resides, and dailies in the larger group by which Ms. Powers was employed for fifteen years.

While her primary market is small newspapers, Ms. Powers will target corporate newsletters and small, regional magazines as well. Through telecommunications and information technology, the real market for this business is nationwide and worldwide.

The Powers Agency aims to add one new client a month in the first year.

The agency will pursue its markets initially through targeted mailings of complete information packets including business card, brochure, fact sheets, and testimonials. The mailing will be followed by personal telephone calls. In addition, the agency will create an electronic web site and follow up telephone calls and brochures with E-mail queries that include a monthly "tip sheet" with a couple of tips for attracting and retaining readers.

[I'll talk more about marketing, and give you a sample marketing plan, in Chapter 6.]

Rate structure

Ms. Powers will base her fee schedule on an hourly rate of $75 in non-metro markets, but will adjust that fee upward in line with the competition in more urban markets. She will price her services with a combination of both hourly rates and total project bids based on the hourly rate, depending on the specific nature of the project.

The competition

Currently, there are no newspaper consultants targeting the small publications that the Powers Agency will target. Other consultants target the larger metropolitan papers and larger national groups, and thus are priced beyond the means of smaller newspapers and publications. This virtual lack of competition provides a real opportunity to market these services to this niche.

Financing

The $8,000 loan will be used as follows:

Computer upgrade	$2,000
Color laser printer	$1,500
Fax machine	$1,000
Office furniture, phone, equipment	$1,500
Marketing materials, promotion	$2,000

The owner's $10,000 will be used for additional start-up costs including an initial advertising campaign, first-year operating expenses and for living expenses.

WHAT ABOUT YOUR FINANCING?

Now that you've drawn up your business plan, it's time to look at your financing. As I pointed out earlier, the beauty of establishing a home-based consulting business is its low cost. You have

Financial plan (first year)

	Jan	Feb	Mar	Apr	May	June	July	Aug	Sept	Oct	Nov	Dec	Total
Projected Revenue	0	$500	$1,000	0	$5,000	$5,000	$5,000	$1,000	$500	$2,000	$6,000	$5,000	$31,000
Operating Expenses													
Rent	0	0	0	0	0	0	0	0	0	0	0	0	0
Debt service	200	200	200	200	200	200	200	200	200	200	200	200	2,400
Supplies	500	100	100	100	100	100	500	100	100	100	100	100	2,000
Telephone	110	100	100	100	110	100	100	100	110	100	100	100	1,230
Postage	40	40	40	40	40	40	40	40	40	40	40	40	480
Marketing and advertising	300	300	300	125	125	125	125	125	125	125	125	125	2,025
Legal and accounting fees	100	100	100	100	100	100	100	100	100	100	100	100	1,200
Insurance	100	100	100	100	100	100	100	100	100	100	100	100	1,200
Miscellaneous	50	50	50	50	50	50	50	50	50	50	50	50	600
Total operating expenses	1,400	990	990	815	825	815	1,215	815	825	815	815	815	11,135
Net Profit (Loss)	(1400)	(490)	10	(815)	4,175	4,185	3,785	185	(325)	1,185	5,185	4,185	19,865

almost no overhead and you don't have to buy inventory. You're carrying your inventory and your equipment on your shoulders, because what you're selling is your expertise and knowledge.

So you may not need financing help. Instead, you may be able to launch your business with savings or even with credit cards. On the other hand, in today's technological age, communications equipment can be costly. You may not want to dip into your savings or your stream of income.

You'll probably have to purchase or upgrade basic office equipment. You'll need an answering machine, copier, fax machine, and computer with word processing, database, and accounting and billing software. If you intend to produce your own promotional materials you should invest in a laser printer and desktop publishing software.

If you buy a modem and telecommunications software you can

tap into on-line information systems that allow you to communicate with clients and other consultants. You can also monitor industry trends and solicit clients in the business and financial areas of the commercial on-line services like CompuServe, Prodigy, and America Online.

You also need money to live on while the business gets rolling, but if you've been downsized, your severance package should provide a few months' worth of living expenses.

For now, start a new worksheet in your business notebook to calculate your start-up costs. Here's what you'll need:

START-UP COSTS WORKSHEET

[Enter the appropriate amounts to determine your overall costs. I've listed some typical expenses, but you should make sure your list is specific for the particular kind of home-based consulting business you're going to start.]

Telephone installation	$_____
Insurance	$_____
Attorney	$_____
Accountant	$_____
Marketing/advertising firm	$_____
Computer	$_____
Modem	$_____
Printer	$_____
Software	$_____
Internet service provider	$_____
Fax machine	$_____
Telephone	$_____
Beeper	$_____
Answering machine	$_____
Furniture	$_____
Copy machine	$_____
File cabinet	$_____
Office supplies	$_____
Stationery	$_____
Total advertising	$_____
Total start-up costs	$_____

Now that you've figured out your start-up costs you need to arrange financing. Basically, you have three options: your own funds, a personal loan from a lending institution, or a loan from family or friends.

Your own funds

If you're a dedicated saver, you may have sufficient savings. Or you may have assets you can convert to cash. Even the simplest consulting business requires an outlay for office supplies. You have to keep records and send out bills, right?

While getting downsized can be traumatic, you may be lucky enough to have come away with a severance package you can invest in starting up your new business. Or maybe you've inherited a little nest egg. That, too, can be an excellent source of financing for your business start-up.

Institutional sources

Forget a business loan. Banks don't lend to start-ups because it's too risky. They want a proven track record before they'll consider a business loan. Your best bets are credit cards, a home equity loan, or a personal loan. Base your choice on how much you need to borrow. If you need only a little, say $2,000 or less, use credit cards. If you need a bit more, between $2,000 and $10,000, take out a personal loan; if you need to borrow a lot, better get a home equity loan.

Provided your credit cards aren't maxed out, they can be an easy, convenient way to finance your start-up purchases. But they'll cost you. While you might get lucky and hit a low introductory interest rate on a new card, be sure to read the fine print to find out when the rate zooms up to the general, out-of-sight level of most credit cards. And there's a limit to how much you can charge on a credit card.

Like credit cards, a personal loan can be easy and convenient. You can also borrow more than with credit cards. And if you shop around, you should be able to do much better on the interest rate.

A home equity loan, or second mortgage, is now a very popular form of financing for all sorts of things, including basic business equipment. Banks like home equity loans because there's little risk involved—if you forfeit, they get your house.

It's a simplification, but if your home is worth $175,000 and your mortgage balance is $75,000, you have $100,000 worth of equity in your home. Generally speaking you can borrow against that equity—usually up to 70 percent of its value—to finance your business needs. Even better, the interest on a home equity loan is usually tax deductible, effectively lowering the cost of the loan.

You should search for a home equity loan and a personal loan exactly like you did for your first mortgage. Comparison shop for the best interest rates at banks, credit unions, and savings and loans.

Small Business Administration

The SBA has a number of different loan programs that your local office can describe in detail. Generally, you must have been rejected by at least three other financial institutions before you can apply for an SBA loan. Minorities and other groups are targeted for SBA assistance. There are also SBA loan guarantee programs that work with local banks to guarantee loans to small businesses. There's usually a long waiting list for SBA loans—and tons of paperwork to plow through before you get one—but they're available.

In fact, the SBA has been making strides in recent years in reducing the amount of paperwork involved in getting an SBA loan, and in making more funds available. Between 1989 and 1995, the volume of business loans guaranteed by the SBA increased from $3 billion to $9 billion. And, according to SBA records, the average loan was for about $250,500 over a period of almost twelve years. About a fifth of those loans went to companies under two years old.

Some of the more popular SBA loan programs include:

• **SBA 7(a) guaranteed loans.** Most SBA loans are made under this program, in which private lenders make loans that are guaranteed up to 80 percent by the SBA. The maximum guaranty of loans exceeding $155,000 is 85 percent. There is no minimum-size loan amount and the SBA can guarantee up to $750,000 of a private sector loan. In addition, the SBA provides special incentives to lenders who provide guaranteed loans of $50,000 or less, which is probably where your loan would fall.

• **SBA micro loans.** These are intended for smaller businesses, like yours, which only need a few thousand dollars. There is about

$70 million in micro loan money available, with a typical loan being about $10,000. The maximum is $25,000.

• **SBA direct loans.** These are loans of up to $150,000 and are available only to those unable to secure an SBA-guaranteed loan. They are also available only to certain categories of borrowers, such as veterans, disabled veterans, handicapped people, and for businesses in low-income or high-unemployment areas.

SBA loans are definitely worth checking into, particularly if you have patience with paperwork or don't want to overtax your credit cards.

Family and Friends

If you're on good terms with your family they can be an excellent source of financing. The same is true of friends. It can be a win-win deal for both parties, because there's a gap between current lending rates and the interest rates institutions are offering on savings accounts, certificates of deposit, and other savings instruments.

Say your sister is a successful doctor who's rolling in money and is always on the lookout for a good investment. Right now she's got $15,000 to invest, and by sheer coincidence, that's exactly how much you've decided you need to borrow to start up your new home-based consulting business.

She doesn't want to deal with mutual funds and other more risky investment instruments. She knows that fixed-rate investments earn around 4.5 percent with a conventional savings account and about 6 percent with most CDs.

Meanwhile, you've discovered that a personal loan will cost you about 10 percent. So there's roughly a 4 percent window of opportunity for you and your sister to make a deal that benefits you both. If she lends you her $15,000 at 8 percent, she'll be getting a better return on her investment than she would otherwise and you'll be getting a loan 2 percent below what's available in the marketplace. You both win.

WHAT'S UP WITH MONICA?

A chance comment by her one and only client—about three months into the start of her new freelance consulting business—

finally set Monica on the right path. She and her client were having lunch to discuss the progress of the project, a complete review and overhaul of the company's compensation and benefits plan.

After the conclusion of their business the client inquired casually how Monica's business was coming. Monica hesitated for only a moment, then decided to be honest. Monica had never been one to lie or beat around the bush, which she suspected might be another reason she hadn't survived the political fight at corporate headquarters.

She told the client that she was struggling and wasn't sure she had what it takes to be an entrepreneur. She said she was confident she knew her business—the business of human resources—but that she wasn't so sure she knew the business of business.

The client asked Monica what kind of business and marketing plan she'd put together and how much she's budgeted for marketing. Monica looked at him blankly. Then she confessed somewhat sheepishly that she didn't have either a business plan or a marketing plan.

When he asked what her accountant and attorney thought about that, she confessed again—she was not only flying by the seat of her pants, she was flying solo, without a team of advisers.

Her client pushed back his chair, signaled for the waiter and ordered two cognacs. He said he didn't ordinarily drink at lunch, but this was going to be an occasion. A celebration, in fact.

Monica asked what they were celebrating, considering she'd apparently just flunked a couple of important business tests. For her client it was simple: They would celebrate the fact that she'd been smart enough and naïve enough to be honest about her lack of business preparation. In return, he said, and because she was very good at the business of human resources, he was going to offer her some advice.

He said that if she took it, he'd expect to see her business flourish. He also predicted that if she didn't, she wouldn't last a year. The advice? Three things:

1. Talk with SCORE volunteers immediately and get their help

2. Draft a business plan

3. Draft a marketing plan

Monica's no fool, even if she was a little slow getting down to business. She took his advice and two months later, after several meetings with the SCORE volunteers and some research at the library, she had written her business and marketing plans. Once again she was on the way.

WHAT ABOUT AARON?

Aaron never talked with SCORE. But then Aaron really didn't need to. All the reading he'd done before he ever started moonlighting had advised him to craft a business plan and a marketing plan, and that's what he did.

He even asked an old friend, a retired bank president, if he would look over the plans, and he agreed. The friend had two criticisms. First, that Aaron needed to reconsider his fee schedule. He felt that Aaron was undervaluing himself and that his business image—not to mention his finances—would suffer because of it.

Second, he suggested that Aaron rethink his marketing plan, which was heavily dependent on costly newspaper advertising that would put a dent in his entrepreneurial fund. He advised Aaron to strategize other, less costly means of making his business known: by networking at Business After Hours events, by doing mailings of his brochure, and by teaching a course at the local community college.

He made one other suggestion. Aaron had decided he would use money from his savings fund—his entrepreneurial fund—to purchase the more sophisticated computer and other office equipment he would need to strike out on his own, as well as to refinish and outfit an office in his basement.

His friend suggested he not seriously deplete that fund just when he was ready to cut his employee umbilical cord and quit his day job. Use that fund as a contingency and a cushion, his friend said, and instead take out a home equity loan. That way, during that feast and famine first year he'd have something to fall back on. So that's what Aaron did.

LOCATION, LOCATION, LOCATION

The sages say the three keys to a good business are location, location, and location. We've been assuming all along that your business will be located at home—that a home-based business is the best way for you to start your new freelance consulting business. I still believe that's the best, cheapest, most cost-effective way to get started. But in Chapter 5 I'll explore that issue more thoroughly, tell you exactly what you need to make it work, and give you a few other options if you decide a home business just isn't right for you.

5

THERE'S NO PLACE LIKE HOME

In some ways, many of America's workers are back where they started—at home. Before the Industrial Revolution, most people worked at home, growing and raising everything they and their families needed to survive. They didn't commute to a different location or distant town to work, their work and their lives were intertwined, at home.

Some of today's workers, for a variety of reasons, again are working at home. Many are telecommuting for distant employers, while others are becoming entrepreneurs based at home. And while it may not be right for everyone, more people every year are discovering the joys of working at home.

Some 20 million businesses nationwide are home-based, according to IDC/LINK, a New York–based market research firm. The number is growing annually by 7 to 8 percent, and is expected to reach almost 30 million by 2001. When you include telecommuters who work for someone else, there are 30 million U.S. households in which someone works at home, one-third more than in 1992.

I believe the smartest, most cost-efficient way to start your free-lance consulting business is to base it at home. But admittedly, working at home doesn't work for everyone. You need to consider the pros and cons and decide whether a home office is right for you. Let's take a look at the advantages and disadvantages. If you decide after reading this chapter that you just don't want to work at home, but prefer to rent space elsewhere, you'll need to go back and adjust your business plan to include that expense and any related commuting expenses.

THE ADVANTAGES OF A HOME-BASED CONSULTING BUSINESS

Certainly working at home has unique advantages. One of the beauties of a home-based consulting business is the ease with which you can launch it. Your attic storage room or basement can be transformed into an office. Hang a discreet sign on your door or post a notice on the Internet and you're in business.

Another advantage is the low cost. Your start-up costs are minimal and so is your overhead. Obviously, you save on office rental and commuting costs when working at home. You'll need appropriate office and computer equipment, but beyond that, most of what you need is carried compactly on your shoulders. In fact, you can spend as little as $4,000 to get started if you buy used computer equipment or if you already own good equipment.

And since you determine your work schedule, you can work as little or as much as you like, at whatever odd times you like. Lynda Ford started out thinking she would run her consulting business part time so she could spend more time with her teenage boys. It hasn't quite worked out that way.

Ford said she's working more hours each week for herself than she worked for her previous employer as a full-time executive. But she does have more time to go to her sons' after-school activities, because she often works until one or two in the morning to finish a project. Those late hours are partly caused by a deadline and her decision to be more available for her kids, but it's also because she's so excited now by what she's doing, she doesn't want to stop.

You can decide how many clients you want and how demanding your daily and weekly schedule should be. If you want to factor in a couple of regular weekly golf leagues, no problem. You'll have the freedom to do just that.

There's also the freedom and pleasure you'll feel from working in an environment you have chosen and designed, and in which you feel most comfortable. At home you'll be able to open a real window and breathe fresh air instead of stale, recirculated, institutional carbon dioxide. You can work in sweats or in the buff if you choose. You can work in comfort and save on costly business clothing at the same time.

Esthetically, it will surely be more pleasing than other options. After all, you decorated your home to suit your needs, tastes, and style. Your home office can be utterly simple and distraction free, or it can reflect your personal taste and style just as your home does. Contrast that to large impersonal office buildings and you'll feel not only more inspired but more in command, more in charge of your work and your life. Being master of your domain will help you feel that you're master of your fate and will foster self-confidence. That sense of self-confidence will be an important factor in your business success.

You also can decide exactly how accessible you want to be to family, friends, and clients during your workday. You can set strict working hours and specific visiting or relaxation hours, or you can be flexible. Again, it's your choice and you can do what works best for you. You can listen to your own personal biorhythms, rather than trying to conform to someone else's concept of what you should do when. If you want to throw in a load of laundry while you work out a client's knotty problem or catch a soap opera while you put stamps on a target mailing, you can do it with impunity. Remember, you're the boss.

Don't forget to keep a strict accounting of the space in your home devoted to your business, as well as your utilities, telephone, cleaning service, and even lawn maintenance. Your accountant will be on top of this, but with a home-based business you'll be able to write off a portion of your household expenses when figuring your taxes.

And while you'll have plenty of stress as an entrepreneur, landing clients and keeping your cash flow plentiful and steady, one thing you won't have to contend with any longer is the stress of commuting long hours to work. While others are out there battling their way to work you'll already be there, on the job, getting a jump on the workday or getting in a few extra minutes of sleep if that's what you need.

THERE ARE ALSO DOWNSIDES

A home-based consulting business sounds like an ideal solution so far, doesn't it? But there are some downsides to consider as well. Let's take a look:

The space problem

Your house may not have an extra room, or basement, ready to be converted into your new office. It would be a bit inconvenient to have to use your bedroom as an office and have to move stacks of files and computer disks every time you're getting ready to go to bed.

The telephone crises

Then there are the telephone snafus. If your telephone rings constantly it's a sign your business is healthy. On the other hand, that could drive your family crazy. Your family's personal calls also could be a stumbling block if a client repeatedly has trouble reaching you. Of course there are solutions to phone problems: answering machines, call waiting, and a second phone line, but it's something to consider.

Staying on top

This is key—perhaps the most critical factor you'll need to analyze. If you're selling yourself as an expert in your field, you need to be on top of the latest developments in that and related fields. Magazines, newspapers, and newsletters will help, but you also need regular contact with your peers, and especially with leaders in the field. Attending seminars, conferences, and trade association meetings will be essential.

You'll also need to make special efforts to have regular contact with your peers, clients, and potential clients, as those contacts no longer will come as naturally. When you work at home, networking is something you really have to work at. The old adage "out of sight, out of mind" can prove all too true, so you'll need to seek out new business contacts aggressively.

The loneliness

Even for people who essentially are loners, the enforced aloneness of working at home can become a problem. You'll have to make an effort to get out of the house and meet people not connected with your business. You may become so obsessed with your new business that you make little time for anything else, and that can begin to be confining and limit your outlook on life and eventually your business perspective.

So be sure to make plans to socialize regularly and then actually do it. Make regular dates to work out at the health club or play tennis or ride horses—whatever gets you out and about with friends and family, not just business acquaintances. Loneliness can be a subtle, slowly debilitating disease that you need to stave off aggressively.

You also might consider teaching an adult education class at the local high school or at the community college. Not only would that help you ward off loneliness, but it could serve another purpose: help you market your expertise, and therefore promote your business. As an entrepreneur, it's great if you can learn to turn negative situations into business opportunities.

Where to meet

It may not be convenient or appropriate to invite clients to your at-home office for business meetings, so you'll have to find a comfortable, reliable, quiet alternative. You may want to join a health club with a café, and kill two birds with one stone—having exercise and a meeting space. Or talk with the owner of a local restaurant about taking a little extra time over lunch once or twice a week. He'll probably be happy for the regular business, and won't object as long as he knows what you're planning ahead of time.

The distractions

This can be a major stumbling block to working at home. You'd better be disciplined if you decide to go for it, because all your favorite toys and your favorite playmates will be there to lure you from your appointed task—the stereo, the TV, your spouse or friend, that new novel you just started and don't want to put down, or a new recipe you're dying to try out.

There definitely will be times when you should be buckling down to business that your home surroundings will call out to you, and you had better be ready to be firm with yourself or risk losing a good client.

These "downsides" to working at home are something you certainly should consider. But consider this, as well. Lynda Ford started her business in one room of her relatively roomy suburban home, then expanded to a second room. At that point her husband said maybe she was outgrowing a home business and suggested she consider leasing space elsewhere.

Ford responded with the same incredulity she'd have felt if he's asked her to fly to the moon. "Are you kidding?" she said. "I love working at home. I love the flexibility, the feeling of comfort. I like being able to work on a project until two in the morning."

She had another suggestion for her husband: "Let's knock down a couple of walls and just add on a bigger office." They're considering that option, as The Ford Group continues to grow.

WHAT YOU NEED TO MAKE IT WORK

Setting up a home office sounds simple, doesn't it? Just pick the room you use least often, clear out the junk, put in a desk and a telephone, and you're ready, right? Think again. That sewing room on the third floor may be the first thought that comes to mind, but if you intend to meet with clients or employees in your home office, the third floor sewing room isn't a good idea. Before you can decide where to locate your home office you have to determine your needs, those of your business, and those of your family as well.

Analyze your environment and space needs

First, you need to decide where to locate your home office. Keep in mind that this office will be the heart of your business, and the place you will be spending a good portion of your life in the coming years. This is the place in which you will be giving birth to and nourishing your new business, so you need to create it with all the care you would a real nursery. First and foremost, it should be comfortable and welcoming. It also should be roomy enough to let you spread out and accommodate whatever equipment you'll need.

But keep in mind as well that this is the place where you will be working to fulfill your business goals, so you need to create the kind of work environment that will stimulate you to continue working on those projects and goals when you'd rather drift off to join the family fun. Your space should also be designed with your particular business needs in mind.

At the same time, of course, you can't forget that your office will be sharing space in your home, so you need to be sensitive to the needs and concerns of other family members as you create your new space.

The most important thing to remember as you start to establish your home office is that the key to working successfully at home is to be able to create both psychological and physical barriers between work and family. If flexibility is one of your goals you can maintain whatever fluidity you wish between the two, but you still must be able to make that distinction, that separation, in order to be able to bring total concentration to the job. That will be a key to your business success.

Now, consider your home objectively and list what you think are the obvious places you could set up shop. Perhaps you have a downstairs guest bedroom you could easily live without. Then there's the basement, which with some work could be habitable. Or that third-floor sewing room. All three sound like possibilities. But before you make any hasty decisions, you need to analyze how the areas around those rooms are used. Remember, your office will be in a home that's used by other members of your family, not in a vacuum and not in a building of other offices.

So ask yourself these questions about your home, those rooms in particular, and about your own work habits:

What rooms are used most each day and what rooms are used least?

What times of day are areas of my home used most?

What's the noise level in various areas of the house, both during the day and in the evening? Particularly, what is the noise level in the rooms immediately adjacent to those on my target list?

Will clients and/or work associates be visiting my office?

Does my business have any unique equipment or space needs?

Do I need total silence to work effectively or is some background noise acceptable?

Do I need a window to feel comfortable?

Do I need plenty of desk and table space to spread out when I work, or do I tend to pack things away, out of sight, as I finish with them?

Answers to these questions should help you to determine the best space for your home office. Be prepared. They may even indicate you need to do some switching of rooms or renovating to make the most appropriate space. For example, say the downstairs guest room would be ideal, but it's next to the family room. The kids use the family room a lot in the afternoons and evening, so the noise level and distractions would be a problem.

The basement is unfinished and much too damp and moldy. Refinishing it is a possibility, particularly as it has an entrance to the outside that could be made usable for clients. But the expense is daunting. And your wife really doesn't like the idea of giving up her sewing room; besides, the room is really too small and dark.

Let's reconsider the first floor. In addition to the guest room and family room, your master bedroom is across the hall. You hadn't considered your bedroom at all, but think again. You could either locate your office in your bedroom and move your bedroom to what's now the guest room or the family room, whichever is largest, and make the other the family room. That keeps your office away from the noise. And when you have a few clients under your belt and the revenue is rolling in, you can reconsider renovating the basement into a full office suite. Or like Lynda Ford, consider adding an addition onto your home.

One note of caution if you need to remodel or renovate right off the bat. Be sure your plans comply with all local building and zoning codes before you start. Your attorney and contractor will be able to counsel you in this regard, but don't take anything for

granted. You also can get this information yourself from the local
building inspector's office or from the zoning board office. Many
municipalities require you to get permits before you do anything
at all to change the structure of your home, or before you add
any structure, even a small shed, to your property.

Start with the basics

Only you can decide exactly what you will need in your office to
accomplish the unique consulting tasks you will undertake. Every
consultant has different needs because every consultant provides
a custom-made menu of services. The more sophisticated and specialized your services, the more sophisticated and specialized the
equipment you will need to provide those services. On the other
hand, there are some basic necessities every consultant needs, so
let's take a look at those first. The configuration of your space
will be determined primarily by what you need to put into it.

Your most basic needs are a work surface—which can be a
desk, table, or drawing board—and a chair. Since you'll be spending a lot of time in the chair and at the work surface you need to
be sure they are comfortable and spacious. If your work surface
is too small you'll be frustrated with constant paper and project
shuffling. You'll also risk inefficiency and the loss of important
documents. You need to be able to spread out without having
things fall on the floor and behind the desk.

In fact, you really need two surfaces if you can swing it in your
space. One for your computer and one to serve as a desktop for
paperwork. That way you don't have to keep clearing things away
to do different tasks.

Your chair should be ergonomically sound and adjustable, so
you can be sure that your body, your chair, and your work surface
interface at the proper heights, with your head, back, and neck at
the appropriate angles. Your back should be straight, with support
at your lower back. Your feet should rest flat on the floor to
minimize fatigue and back strain.

Great strides have been made in ergonomically designed furniture in the last several years, and the right choices can help ensure
you don't develop painful conditions such as carpal tunnel syndrome (also known as repetitive stress syndrome). Just as it would

be foolish to buy a used car without proper safety features in order to save a few bucks, it would be "penny-wise and pound-foolish" to begrudge the extra bucks it will cost for good office furniture. The money you save won't make up for the cost of future doctor bills if you pinch pennies here.

If you aren't sure what constitutes "ergonomically sound" furniture for you, consult staff at a good office supply store. Their salespeople have been trained to help you determine what's right for your body type, so pick their brains and then shop around for the right price.

Some manufacturers produce specialized workstations designed for home offices, with a computer storage section and pull-out keyboard shelf. Many close up to look like cabinets. You just need to be sure that when you type your elbows are at right angles with your wrists' level, not with your hands bent up. If your keyboard is too high, lower it or raise your chair. But your feet also should rest flat on the floor, so if raising your chair means your feet dangle, as mine do, get a footrest.

On your desk or table, of course, you'll need a telephone, Rolodex for important telephone numbers, and desk supplies. You also need good storage space for documents, files, and projects. You'll probably need several file cabinets in addition to whatever drawer space your desk may have. Shelves lining one or several walls are also a good idea and increase your ability to keep your mind and work space less cluttered.

Good lighting is very important, both for the health of your eyes and for your psyche. Working in a perpetual gloom can make you, well, gloomy, and that doesn't help when you have to deal with clients. It's best if you have a good source of natural light, from either a window or a skylight, although some people find a window too distracting. You'll need a good desk lamp, in addition to any ceiling fixtures the room may have. Some people like bright fluorescent lighting, but I prefer softer, homier lights. Many people actually find they get headaches from fluorescent lights. Just be sure you don't put your monitor facing or opposite a window, as the glare and reflection will hurt your eyes.

That pretty much covers the basics you'll need for your home office. Of course, many people today consider a computer and other high-tech equipment basic for any office, home or otherwise. Let's see what technology can do for you.

Technology can help you do the work of ten

Depending on your business, that may be a slight exaggeration, but not by much. Technology is such a basic part of business life today that we sometimes forget how wonderful and time-saving it can be. But think about it. A fax machine with speed dial and memory can be programmed to send a mailing to ten or fifty potential clients, letting you get on with the creative problem solving you need to do, and without the need for a costly office employee. Or you can program your computer to send those faxes. An answering machine or voice mail can save you numerous costly interruptions to your concentration. And if you establish at the outset that you religiously return those client calls within the same day, even clients who hate voice mail will continue to call.

As just about everybody knows by now the race along the information superhighway is taking us places we never even knew existed before and making it much easier and faster to get there. Technology is the vehicle that has allowed home-based entrepreneurs not only to enter the race but to compete effectively in the business world.

Chances are from your years in the corporate world you're already used to working on a computer. But you probably had someone else, a technology department for example, purchase your computer, set it in front of you, and plug it in. Now you're going to have to be your own tech department and select your equipment yourself. Yes, there's a dizzying array to choose from, but don't despair, and don't assume you have to get too fancy. You're outfitting a home office, not AT&T, and at the start all you'll need are the basics.

You'll probably need two dedicated phone lines, a good fax machine, a reasonably high-powered computer, a good laser or ink jet printer, some software programs, an answering machine or voice mail, and perhaps a photocopier. Of course, you'll also need a modem and telecommunications software so you can tap into on-line information systems and communicate with clients via electronic mail.

You're probably looking at an investment in the $5,000 to $10,000 range, depending on the quality of equipment you purchase and whether it's new or used. Of course, if you need special equipment for graphic design or whatever, you can count on spending more.

But thanks to The Small Business Job Protection Act signed by President Clinton in 1996, you can deduct up to $17,500 worth of capital purchases each year, instead of depreciating it over a number of years. And under the bill, the amount will gradually increase to $25,000.

Deciding what technology to buy

To gain the full benefit of computer technology you must know what to choose and how to use it efficiently. And that involves much more than turning a computer on and typing a letter.

The right hardware and software can mean doing in minutes what used to take hours, or even days. It also can be an easy, efficient, direct lifeline to your client. First, however, you'll need to identify the specific technology that will help your business. When evaluating the range of options, weigh the merits of each against these considerations:

Will the tool or service enable me to make more productive use of my time?

Will it enable me to do a better job of what I'm already doing?

Can I use it to broaden my reach in the marketplace?

Does it improve client service by reducing response time or giving clients better access to me?

Will the technology pay for itself in cost savings, increased productivity, or expanded revenue-producing opportunities?

It's important to tailor the technology mix to your business operation. List every task your business performs during a given day, and consider whether technology can help you accomplish that task more efficiently or productively. Only invest in the tools for which you have a proven use. Then expand your capabilities as your needs evolve.

If you're not sure whether a specific technology will help you, do some experimenting. Most reputable computer and office equipment companies will offer free demonstrations and trials. Why invest in anything when you're not sure it offers the solutions you need? For telecommunications services such as a toll-free 800 number, conference calling, and E-mail, it's easy and inexpensive to experiment with your options. Sign up for these services and track the results for a couple of months. If they're effective, keep the service; if not, cancel it.

With hardware, the upfront investment is more substantial. And there's always the likelihood this year's breakthrough will be quickly outdated. If you're watching your budget, leasing equipment at first may make more sense than outright purchase. Try now, buy later: It's an inexpensive way to sample technology before its benefits are proven.

But if you decide to buy, do it right. Mapping out your expectations will simplify your job. Then just match software and hardware to your needs. Watch out for a few common pitfalls, and you'll be fine. Here are some pitfalls to avoid:

• **The biggest mistake.** People often buy hardware, then try to decide what to do with it. This is definitely the wrong way to go. It's more important to decide which software meets your needs, then choose hardware that will run it.

• **Cost versus price.** When comparing systems, make sure it's apples to apples. The price of one system often seems higher, but when the cost of its extra features are considered, it may be a better deal. Also consider future expansion—can you add peripherals with ease, or do you need costly expansion cards to control them?

• **Beware of software packages.** Many systems come with large software packages; that's often a good thing, but be careful. Packages are often used to make it seem like a better deal than it really is. Check the actual retail price of the programs included to determine their value. More important, is it software you'll use?

• **Monitor myths.** Contrast and clarity are important. You're going to be staring at this thing for a long time. Make sure you can read the display. Consider a larger screen if you'll be doing any sort of design or page layout. The time saved in scrolling around alone will be worth the extra cost, but make sure your computer can handle it.

Finding the correct combination of hardware and software may require specialized knowledge and expertise. Just as it often makes sense to stick to your own area of expertise—running your business—and hire legal and tax advisers, it often makes sense to hire a technology adviser: a computer consultant.

Finding a computer consultant

The best way to find a computer consultant is through personal recommendations. Ask other small business owners and management consultants for suggestions. In addition, most hardware and software companies maintain lists of consultants knowledgeable about their products. Contact companies whose products you're considering and ask for their recommendations.

Then, check computer magazines. There are probably ads for computer consultants in the back. Telephone those listed and ask about their clients, services, and credentials. If you discover they're geared toward servicing larger firms, ask if they have any suggestions for consultants who service small home-based businesses.

When you have a list of candidates, interview those who look most promising. But remember, you're in charge. Don't let the consultant intimidate you with technological jargon. She may be responsible for one of the most important elements of your business, so she must be able to explain her business in language that you can understand. That's her job.

If you don't understand something, ask. If she can't explain something in language you understand, find another consultant. The problem isn't just going to disappear and is bound to get worse when equipment and software arrives.

The consultant must understand your business and work flow, so have specific scenarios in mind which you can discuss. Before she arrives for her interview, outline your average workday. Then list every task your business needs to perform, so she can understand the scope of your needs.

Experience in your particular business is good, but not essential. The ability to react quickly and solve problems is just as, if not more, important. In addition, broad-based experience in other businesses could bring solutions you'd never have thought of.

Make sure the person you're interviewing will be the person actually performing the work. Discuss availability and access in emergencies. Will the consultant be available on weekends and evenings? Can she be paged? Are there surcharges for emergency service? Ask if you'll be billed for all telephone calls.

Independent research can save you a great deal of money. Most consultants will supply you with hardware and software, but you should know the actual consumer price of anything you're going to buy from a consultant.

You have a right to know a consultant's markup. Most will provide itemized invoices and charge a fee (based on their hourly rate) for research and the selection of equipment. If a consultant won't tell you her markup or won't provide itemized bills, there's a reason. Cross her off your list.

Hourly rates usually are linked to the scope and duration of the job and are generally negotiable. The more you'll be using the consultant's services, the less you can expect to pay per hour.

Finally, make this a win-win situation. If you're pleased with the service you're receiving, offer to serve as a reference. Such a vote of confidence can result in even better service. And maybe you can get her to carry your business card with her as well, to drop on the desk of any potential clients she encounters.

There's more to your office than a computer

Once you've got your computer system nailed down, you need to outfit the rest of your office. Here's a rundown on the other equipment you'll need:

Printer. Unquestionably, the highest-quality documents are produced by laser printers. You're in luck, because they've gotten better in speed and resolution while the price has dropped in recent years. Today, you can get sharper text at up to six pages a minute for about $350. If you need to produce higher volumes, you may want a printer that produces eight pages or more a minute, but be prepared to spend a lot more.

Dot matrix printers are the cheapest and most economical to run, and are fine for draft copies or internal use. Not for client copies. Ink jet copiers are less expensive than laser printers, but can be just as expensive to run. Their text isn't as sharp and can smudge.

If you need to produce color documents you can get either an ink jet or laser printer. The ink jet versions are slower but cheaper. If you only foresee needing color documents occasionally you may find it cheaper to have them printed commercially.

Telephone. You need ready access to your clients, and they'll want you within quick calling distance: at the other end of the phone. You could try to get by with one line, but I wouldn't recommend it. Yes, you can get a low-cost electronic device that allows you to operate your phone, fax machine, and computer modem through a single line, but you won't be able to make or receive calls while sending or receiving a fax or checking your E-mail. That limitation will ultimately hurt your business; two lines are a good investment.

You may also need a phone capable of handling more than one call at a time, with a hold button. Extras like a multinumber memory, speed dialing, and caller ID can mean greater efficiency and help business but certainly aren't a necessity. You may find a headset helpful for freeing your hands to take notes, however. And naturally, your business phone should have a number different from your home number to maintain a professional appearance.

Voice mail or answering machine. If you don't expect to get too many calls, an inexpensive answering machine can work. But most home machines have a poor sound quality that can hurt your professional image. Most telephone companies now offer voice mail service for about $15 a month. If your line is busy the call is routed to an electronic mailbox and a sound or lighted button on your telephone lets you know a message is waiting.

Fax machine. There's no question you must have a fax machine, as the fax is now a standard form of business communication.

You won't be taken seriously as a consultant if you don't invest in a fax machine. The good news is it's no longer a major investment. For about $400 you can get a good fax machine that uses easy-to-handle, plain copy paper, rather than the old-style, tissuey thermal paper that was so hard to handle.

But you may want some extra features that can push the price up a bit. Basic features you need include line in/line out, automatic transmission, and a multipage document feed. But if you'll be transmitting documents to many clients regularly, you may want a machine with a large telephone number memory and automatic polling and broadcast features for transmitting documents after normal business hours.

Definitely try out any fax machine before you buy it to ensure it offers the features and quality reproduction you want. And if you're purchasing a new computer, it may have built-in fax capabilities.

Photocopier. Unfortunately, the price of photocopy machines hasn't dropped as much as printers, though they have come down a bit. If your volume is low you may be able to get away with what's called a personal, or home, copier. You can get one of those for about $700. If you only need an occasional copy for your own use, you can probably get by with a copy from your fax machine. But if your volume is high, you'll need a business quality copier, and that will cost you at least $1,500. Or, you can check into the possibily of leasing a copier.

The all-in-one machine. Relatively new on the market is a hybrid machine that combines printing, photocopying, and faxing capabilities in one machine. You can get one based on ink jet technology for about $700, or on laser technology for about $1,000. Just be sure it has the speed and capacity you need before you put your money down. And remember the old adage: A jack of all trades is a master of none.

There are a host of other gizmos you can get into if you have the cash and the fancy for new gadgets: cell phones, portable computers, pagers, and all kinds of business accounting, organizing, and scheduling software. But the line-up above will get you off to a good start. All the high-tech gizmos in the world won't ensure business success unless you put them to good use.

Your home office equipment shopping list

Use this list simply as a guide in shopping for equipment for your home office. You may not need or want everything on the list, or you may need something not listed. But I suggest that you purchase absolutely nothing until you review the list, determine exactly what you need, and check out specific products and prices. Happy shopping.

Equipment/Item	Essential	Cost	Extra
Computer system	_____	_____	_____
portable	_____	_____	_____
desktop	_____	_____	_____
processor speed	_____	_____	_____
amount of RAM	_____	_____	_____
hard drive size	_____	_____	_____
upgrade capability	_____	_____	_____
Modem	_____	_____	_____
CD-ROM drive	_____	_____	_____
Printer	_____	_____	_____
Dot matrix	_____	_____	_____
Ink jet	_____	_____	_____
Laser	_____	_____	_____
Color	_____	_____	_____
Other peripherals	_____	_____	_____
scanner	_____	_____	_____
digital camera	_____	_____	_____
external drives	_____	_____	_____
Software	_____	_____	_____
word processing	_____	_____	_____
database	_____	_____	_____
financial management	_____	_____	_____
contact management	_____	_____	_____
schedule management	_____	_____	_____
presentation	_____	_____	_____

Equipment/Item	Essential	Cost	Extra
desktop publishing	___	___	___
graphics	___	___	___
Other specialty software	___	___	___
Telephone system	___	___	___
multi line phone	___	___	___
call waiting	___	___	___
call forwarding	___	___	___
caller ID	___	___	___
voice mail	___	___	___
hold button	___	___	___
auto redial	___	___	___
number memory/speed dial	___	___	___
conference calling	___	___	___
Answering machine	___	___	___
multiple messages	___	___	___
remote retrieval	___	___	___
remote messaging	___	___	___
Fax machine	___	___	___
auto document load	___	___	___
receive memory	___	___	___
multinumber memory	___	___	___
automatic redialing	___	___	___
polling	___	___	___
delayed transmission	___	___	___
automatic transmission	___	___	___
Photocopier	___	___	___
color	___	___	___
oversized pages	___	___	___
reduction	___	___	___
enlargement	___	___	___
Pager/cell phone	___	___	___
Estimated costs	___	___	___

This list should help you get started equipping your home office. Or, for that matter, any office space you choose, whether it's located in your home or elsewhere. After all, sometimes, despite the seeming logic and savings associated with locating your business in your home, it just doesn't appear it'll work out. What then?

IF HOME JUST WON'T WORK

If you have to lease or rent space for your consulting business there are several things to keep in mind as you select your space. First and foremost are location and image. If you're going to spend money to rent your space you'll want to get the most out of it. That means it should be appropriate not only as a place to house you, your equipment and any associates or employees, it also should be the kind of space to which you can bring clients.

The location should be convenient. If you have to give a client directions that sound like winding your way through a maze, you run the risk of having that client decide it's just too much trouble to find your office. What you don't need is high public visibility, which can be quite costly. A business consultant doesn't depend on walk-in traffic but rather on good marketing, promotion, and word of mouth.

In addition to being convenient, your location and the office itself must offer a professional image. A client's perception of you and confidence in you can alter subtly but irreparably if your office appears less than professional.

You don't want to be located in a rundown section of the city or near a bar or nightclub, for example, even if the price is right. And not at the rear of a Laundromat, either. Examine any possible office space carefully before you lease, and check out the surrounding neighborhood. The best kind of space for a consulting business is in an office building with other professional offices.

Don't forget to analyze any space with future expansion needs in mind. Ask yourself, is there room to expand and if so, how costly would it be to do so? And don't forget to call in your attorney to review and negotiate any commercial lease before you sign it. Most real estate brokers are working for the landlord and aren't concerned about you and the kind of deal you're getting. You need your own attorney to be an advocate for you in this process.

Make sure your lease has renewal options that extend at least as far as your break-even point. It's also a good idea to get a short lease with numerous renewal options. That gives you the best of both possible worlds. You can leave after a relatively short time if you need to, but you have the option to stay if the space works well.

If your business is incorporated, and it should be, the lease should be signed by your corporation, not by you as an individual. That will insulate you from any personal liability if the business should fail. Also, be sure you are paying only for carpetable space, not for other kinds of square footage, such as space under or outside the walls. Carefully check what other kinds of charges are included, such as lobby space, air-conditioning, and other pass-alongs. You don't want to pay dearly or unfairly for the fine print in your lease.

Your lease should be assignable and should stipulate that the location can be used for any other legal use or for general use by any business similar to yours. That can help ensure you flexibility if you decide to move your business; the landlord won't be able to make you carry out the full length of the lease personally.

Make sure you understand under what terms the landlord has the right to cancel the lease and that you receive appropriate remuneration. Rent increases should be outlined in detail in terms of both amount and timing. If renovation work is required, be sure to include that in the lease. Try to delay rent payment until all work is completed.

Remember, the terms of all leases are negotiable. Both you and the landlord are in business, and effective negotiation of the lease is a simple business proposition. But that negotiation, and the location of your space, can either contribute to your future business success or create unending problems for your business. Proceed carefully and thoughtfully in selecting and negotiating your space.

MORE ABOUT MONICA AND AARON

For both Monica and Aaron, the decision to base their businesses at home was a no-brainer. The cost effectiveness of a home office was the deciding factor, as neither had the cash to lay out for commercial rent on top of the start-up equipment costs they would have to incur. Both needed to go on a shopping spree to outfit their home offices, but that would be a small price to pay compared with renting or leasing and then equipping an outside business location.

By this time Aaron had more business than he could conveniently handle, while working a full-time, professional day job. He'd been consulting part time for almost nine months and was feeling pulled in two different directions. There really wasn't much time for sleep. He decided it was time to go cold turkey—almost. He felt it was only fair to give his boss three months notice so he could find and train a replacement without feeling rushed. That would also give Aaron more time to shift his home office from a corner of his bedroom to a suite in the basement.

Before he could do that, though, Aaron needed to have some renovation work done to make his unfinished basement habitable— and presentable—as an office. He also wanted to install an extra window to improve the lighting and an entrance to the outside to give clients easy access so they wouldn't have to troop through his family's living space. He figured the renovations wouldn't come cheap, but he wanted this home office to work well for his family, his clients, and him. He was willing to spend some money to do it right.

His contractor estimated he could get the job done decently— not luxuriously—for $20,000. Aaron estimated he'd need another $10,000 to $15,000 for computer upgrades, a new laser printer, a fax machine, and small copier as well as cabinets, desk and ergonomic chair, lamps, and an answering machine. And a phone and a couple of phone lines.

He decided he didn't have the patience to try the Small Business Administration loan programs so he opted for a $40,000 home equity loan. He hoped that it would give him an extra $5,000 or so for his contingency fund. He was really worried about those famine months he expected down the road.

Monica already had a small computer room, which she shared with her teenagers and her husband, on the first floor of her home. While not ideal—it was too close to the TV room and the kitchen— she decided it would have to do as an office for the present. The kids mostly played games or surfed the Net on the three-year-old computer, so she decided to give it to them—it could go in the TV room or a bedroom. She would buy a new state-of-the art computer and laser printer for herself.

She figured the only other items she needed to purchase immediately were a fax machine, an answering machine, another phone and a couple of business phone lines, and a good, ergonomic chair. Her desk was old but solid and serviceable, as were the file cabinets already in the room. Maybe a new lamp.

She figured she could get by with spending $4,000 to $5,000, and she could do that on a new credit card with a very low first-year interest rate. She didn't want to blow the remaining $10,000 of her severance, since that would have to be her contingency fund.

Once Monica and Aaron had their purchases planned, their home offices were almost as good as ready. And so were they. It was time to get down to business—almost.

GETTING DOWN TO BUSINESS

So you've got your business planned and you've got your office— home or otherwise—located and equipped. Now you're ready for Part Two, Covering Your Bases, which will give you the nitty-gritty on how to get, keep, and deal with clients, how to market and promote your business, and how to ensure success. You're almost as good as there.

Part Two

•

COVERING
YOUR
BASES

6

SECURING CLIENT
NUMBER TWO

It's often easy to land your first client. Some consultants start with their current or former employer, or with clients they worked with while they were still employed. Many consultants who start out part time while still employed don't take the challenging step of jumping into the water full time until they have several clients.

But say you've been downsized and started your business with just one contract to consult for your former employer. The job market looks grim and besides, you really want to be your own boss. Like Lynda Ford, you really don't want to work for anyone else. And you're confident you can make it on your own.

The big question is, How to secure client number two? And three? And four? Assuming you are good at what you do, don't worry. There are simple and effective marketing techniques that will help you get the job done.

You touched on marketing in your business plan, but you will need to develop a separate marketing plan to detail exactly how you'll promote your consulting business for at least a year. Marketing shouldn't be a hit-or-miss proposition or something you think about as time permits. Make time, and make a plan. I'll give you a sample marketing plan to use as a guide later in this chapter. If you want your business to be successful, you have to market yourself.

WHAT IS MARKETING, ANYWAY?

Thomas L. Greenbaum is president of Groups Plus, Inc., a focus group research and consulting firm, and teaches a consulting course at Harvard University. In his classic text, *The Consultant's Manual,* he defined what he considers to be a marketing mix especially appropriate for a consulting business. He called it ''The Nine Ps of Marketing a Consulting Service,'' and described it this way:

> *The consultants' marketing mix can be visualized as a bicycle wheel: The successful practice is the axle, and the various parts of the mix are the spokes. For the wheel to turn, each of the spokes must contribute to the functioning of the whole. If one spoke is weak, the wheel will not work effectively to propel the axle forward. The key to successful marketing of a consulting practice is to ensure that all elements of the mix are developed carefully and working at peak effectiveness.*

These are Greenbaum's nine *P*s, the elements of his special consulting marketing mix:

1. Planning. This part consists of setting the direction for your business, including the services you will offer, the business structure, business plan, and financial elements of the business. It also involves determining your target market and potential clients.

2. Price. This element consists of your fee structure, which I discussed in Chapter 4.

3. Place. This category is about where your business is located. I discussed the importance of choosing the location of your home office, as well as the location of rented office space, in Chapter 5.

4. Packaging. This idea refers to the image your business presents through graphic materials such as business cards, brochures, presentation materials, and stationery. It also includes the image you and your office present. In business, image is all about packaging and presentation, and you want your image to be one of confident professionalism.

5. Positioning. Greenbaum says ''Positioning of the consulting practice establishes how you want your business to be viewed by the client/prospect population. In essence, the positioning is the personality and character of the business.''

6. People. This concept refers to the types of clients you are seeking to attract, the personality traits and quality of those you might employ in the business, as well as your own personality and people skills.

7. Product. The product consists not only of the services your consulting business offers, but also the benefits your business provides in terms of your credentials, professional skills, and achievements.

8. Promotion. Promotion incorporates the four key traditional marketing functions, including: paid advertising; paid promotional materials sent directly to the target client; public relations efforts, including events and the use of unpaid media to attract interest among prospective clients; sales, including sales calls, presentations, development of the proposal, and follow-up after the sales call.

9. Professionalism. Professionalism relates not only to the image you project but to every aspect of the way you conduct and carry out your business, including your day-to-day operations and your ethical standards. It also extends to you and your business's involvement in community activities.

All *P*s aside, never for a moment forget: As a freelance consultant, you are the business, and the best way to build your business is to build your reputation. Your name and reputation are your most important business assets. And there's no question that the best and most cost-effective advertising is through word of mouth. A satisfied client is money in the bank, and the more of them you have out there in the business community, the more the good word about your business will spread.

The key to effective marketing is to keep your name in front of clients and potential clients as much as possible, in as many ways as possible. The biggest mistake most small businesses make is to rely on advertising. Advertising is the most expensive and often least productive way to reach clients. Instead, you'll want to spread your efforts among a variety of marketing opportunities.

Keep in mind, too, that marketing isn't something you do just once a month in a particular time slot, like paying the bills. Marketing should permeate your life. Just about everything you do should, in one way or another, become a marketing opportunity.

Marketing tricks you can try

You definitely should check in regularly with current clients and former clients to see how they're doing and whether they need additional help. The idea is to make it very easy for them to remember and reach out to you. But beyond that, and in addition to some targeted advertising and standard marketing brochures, here are some things to try out and work into your marketing plan:

Teach a course. Teaching can help establish your credentials as well as your name recognition. Try teaching at the local adult education center, community college, or even at the major college level.

Write books and articles. Offer to write a free column for the business section of the local newspaper or a regional business magazine. Write for trade journals. Turn your experience and expertise into a book to help others.

Make presentations. As you establish your credentials through books and articles, these will probably lead to speaking engagements and additional business. Take any opportunity you can to present yourself, your ideas, and your business to as many people as possible, even if at first glance the audience doesn't appear rich with future clients. Word of mouth often works in mysterious ways.

Network, network, network. Keep in touch with industry trends and people in the industry, including former clients, classmates, professors, and coworkers. Join and attend professional associations, workshops, and seminars. You might even take a class from competitors to see what they're up to. This will help you to stay ahead of new trends and to continually update and expand your skills. Also, enter all business contests offered by the professional and business associations. If you win any awards, you can use them as opportunities to promote your business through a local and even national advertising blitz.

Don't forget: You are your greatest business asset, so you need to keep nurturing that asset and to let other professionals know it's growing.

Become active in the community.   Attend community events, Chamber of Commerce meetings, and Business After Hours social groups. Join Rotary, the Parent Teacher Association at your child's school, or the board of directors of the local symphony. Make sure you're seen at, and become actively involved in, any group or event for which people gather. The more prospective clients see you as a well-rounded, active, involved human being—one they're beginning to recognize beyond the business context—the more likely they are to turn to you when their business needs a consultant's help.

Check trade and local publications.   Read these publications regularly to stay ahead of trends and identify potential clients and associates. Look for people who are involved in work that complements your niche specialty. Make an effort to call and meet these people for possible future clients or referrals.

Create a newsletter.   Update clients, former clients, and potential clients about what you're doing and what's happening in your industry and theirs that might have an impact on their business. Keep it short and to the point, with informative, useful information, not long dense text. No one has time for long discourses these days.

Lynda Ford said she spent at least half of her time her first year on marketing, including most of the activities listed above. And she's proud that as her business multiplied in the second half of the year, most of the business was repeat business and referrals. For Ford, client satisfaction, reputation, and word of mouth are marketing wonders.

Her best advice on marketing? "Make sure you do some kind of networking thing every single week, whether it's Rotary, Business After Hours, or professional groups."

Ford said she's definitely gotten more active in the community since she started her business. Those activities include volunteering on boards, the Cancer Society, fund-raisers, and even golf tournaments. It isn't all work and no play, after all. And Ford said all this activity, in addition to increasing her name recognition and bringing in business, has given her a greater sense of the resources her community has to offer.

THE FIRST CONTACT

First impressions count as much in business as they do in other aspects of life, and that means a lot. Making good first impressions is part of marketing, too. You're going to have to woo clients. You no longer have the security of working for an employer who automatically provides you with your clients, so you can't take anything for granted. And your first contact with a prospective client will provide him or her with a lasting impression of you and your business. Make it count.

Often your first contact will be over the telephone. Be sure you have effective, appropriate equipment for handling your calls, including an answering machine or voice mail and sufficient phone lines. But in addition to the proper hardware, be conscious of how you sound when you answer the phone.

Be careful about the unspoken messages you are sending. A gruff "Powers here," no matter how stressed or pressed for time you are, won't help business. No matter how many telephone solicitations you've endured, be sure you sound pleasant, self-assured, and helpful. The call you're about to answer may be a $1 million contract. If your niece is shrieking in the background you may suddenly find yourself listening to a dial tone.

The same goes for that first face-to-face contact. You may be working at home, but consider whether you want to run the risk of answering your front door at 11 A.M. with your hair in rollers, wearing dirty jeans and a laundry basket in your arms. If it's an impetuous prospective client with a $1 million contract in her pocket, you could be in trouble—she may be tempted to pretend she rang the wrong doorbell.

If none of those deadly scenarios takes place and the prospective client introduces herself and settles in to discuss her business needs, be prepared to explain succinctly:

- What services you can offer her.
- Why she should choose you to provide those services.
- How you are qualified to offer those services.
- The cost of those services in relation to their value and the competition.
- Your personal reputation, trustworthiness, and character references.

Also, be prepared to offer her striking, professional-looking printed materials that repeat what you're telling her, reinforce it, and provide additional background material and testimonials.

In fact, your printed materials, such as your business card or brochure, may be the first contact a prospective client has with your business. You want those materials to be professional and striking, but also to give a sense, both graphically and subliminally, of what you're all about.

Keep the text short, simple and direct, though of course not simpleminded. On the business card spell out in a sentence what your business does and what it offers clients. In the brochure, repeat the message about what your business does in one or two sentences, but then list specific services. Then briefly outline your experience, credentials, and achievements, including a few projects completed for satisfied clients. If you've got a testimonial or two, include them, as well as a professional photo of yourself.

Once you provide the prospective client with the information and materials she needs to determine whether she will hire you, don't let her walk out the door or hang up the telephone before she provides you with the following information in return:

- Her name, and how and when she prefers to be contacted.
- The exact nature and location of her business. How long she has been in business.

- How she heard about your consulting business.
- What else she needs to know in order to make a decision on whether to hire you.

In addition to seeking this specific information, you also should use the conversation as an opportunity to establish a bond with the prospective client. Show her you know what questions to ask and what information to provide, but moreover, that you can listen well. If you've heard good things about her business say so, but only if you can be sincere. Don't fake it and don't be obsequious.

If you have acquaintances in common you may mention them briefly. The more you can individualize and personalize yourself the better bond you will establish. But again, don't cross the line and be too familiar or personal. This is a potential business relationship, not a personal one.

Make sure this first contact leaves her with a positive impression—that you're a confident, competent, organized professional and that her business will be in good hands if it's in yours. Marketing is about selling yourself as well as your business, and this is your first opportunity to do just that, so make the most of it.

PAID ADVERTISING CAN BE USEFUL

Newspaper advertising can be outrageously expensive, but can be effective if used on a consistent schedule—though not necessarily frequently—rather than hit or miss. Most homes and business still get a newspaper either daily or weekly.

An ad twice a month in the business section of the Sunday paper, for example, may be worth considering, at least on a trial basis for three to six months. If you monitor where your clients first hear about you, you'll know pretty soon if the newspaper ad is paying off. You'll want to be sure your ad is noticeable, that it stands out, and that it conveys a good sense of your professionalism and the nature of the services you offer. The good news is newspaper ads come in all sizes. Of course, if it's too small, you run the risk that it may not stand out.

You can also consider placing your ad in the classified section of the newspaper. Those ads are less expensive than display ads and many people regularly peruse the classifieds.

Some newspapers offer discounts if you contract for a certain number of column inches of advertising for a year. It's worth investigating. And don't forget to check out how and where your competition is advertising. You may want to match their ads, or go one better.

Don't forget about the Yellow Pages and other local telephone directories, either. Many people looking for businesses of all kinds, including consulting businesses, let their fingers do the walking. You can opt for just a straight listing or go for the more noticeable boxed ad, depending on how much you want to spend and what the competition is doing. But a Yellow Pages listing is a must.

GETTING REPEAT BUSINESS, TESTIMONIALS AND REFERRALS

The best way to get repeat business is to go after it. After a project is complete you should make a point to call the client a few weeks later to be sure he or she is satisfied with the job and to determine whether any loose ends have surfaced.

Also use that call as an opportunity to mine for new business. Ask the client what services he or she might need in the coming year; whether there are any projects coming up that would suit your skills; and if you could make a presentation for those projects or bid on them.

The same rule holds true for getting referrals and testimonials, which are personal letters from clients extolling your services and performance that you can print in your brochure or hand to prospective clients. That rule is, You don't get anything if you don't ask for it.

If you have a satisfied client, ask him to refer your company to his associates who may need consulting services. Give clients a stack of your business cards to keep handy for when such discussions occur. And they do occur. That's how many business deals are made and partnerships occur: by word of mouth from a satisfied customer to one who needs your services.

And it doesn't hurt to ask the satisfied client to go further: to write a testimonial letter on your behalf. Writing a testimonial sometimes takes more time and trouble than a busy executive has available, so volunteer to draft a letter yourself that the client can edit as he sees fit. Make it as easy as possible for your satisfied clients to help you market your business.

DRAFT YOUR MARKETING PLAN

As you draw up your marketing plan, focus on the portrait of your target client that we drew in Chapter 3. Think about ways and places to reach that target client, then decide:

What mix of marketing you will do every week, every month, or seasonally.

How much money you will budget for each marketing effort in that period.

How and by whom that marketing effort will be carried out.

How you will assess the effectiveness of your marketing plan.

Keep in mind that while your marketing techniques should be well thought out and your materials professional in appearance, they don't need to be sophisticated, overly expensive, or high tech in the beginning. For example, simple mailed announcements of your new business to targeted clients can get you started. You can follow up with a personal appearance to drop off complete information packets.

Think about your clients as people, and analyze where they spend their time. This can be church, the health club, a neighborhood association, the country club, or Rotary and Chamber of Commerce meetings. One strategy can be as simple as posting your business card on the bulletin board at the supermarket or local latte café. Find ways to reach them wherever they can be found.

SAMPLE MARKETING PLAN

The Powers Agency provides a full range of human resource services, acting as human resource director, for small companies.

GOALS

- To formally launch the Powers Agency September 30.
- To continue to attract new clients the first year after the launch through varied marketing, promotion, and advertising techniques.

SEPTEMBER

Direct Marketing:
- Prepare and send invitations to opening reception.
- Plan and prepare party for clients, potential clients, community business and political leaders and vendors. [$1,500]

Advertising:
- Contract for twice-weekly local newspaper ads for month of September, October, November as trial. [$800]
- Buy Yellow Pages ad. [$500]

Publicity:
- Send press release and photo to local papers and magazines about new business. [$50]
- Follow with calls suggesting business feature story for Sunday paper.

Networking:
- Attend monthly Business After Hours meeting. [$10]
- Join Chamber of Commerce. [$500]
- Accept invitation to join Board of Directors of Community Arts Partnership.
- Volunteer to serve on United Way fund drive board.

OCTOBER

Direct Marketing:
Send letter and information brochure to target client list. [$400]

Advertising:
Run twice-weekly local newspaper ads for month of October. [$800]

Promotion:
Speak to downtown business group about human resources trends, issues.

Networking:
- Attend monthly Business After Hours meeting. [$10]
- Attend Chamber of Commerce meeting.
- Serve on United Way fund drive board.
- Join Rotary. [$250]
- Attend Community Arts Partnership board meeting.

NOVEMBER

Direct marketing:
- Send newsletter to clients and prospective clients on HR issues, trends. [$300]
- Make follow-up calls to prospective clients sent letter.

Advertising:
Run twice-weekly local newspaper ads for month of November as trial. [$800]

Publicity:
Do free monthly column for local newspaper on HR trends, issues.

Networking:
- Attend monthly Business After Hours meeting. [$10]
- Attend Chamber of Commerce meeting.
- Attend Rotary.
- Attend Community Arts Partnership board meeting.

DECEMBER

Advertising:
Run ad in monthly regional business magazine. [$300]

Publicity:
Do free monthly column for local newspaper on HR trends, issues.

Networking:
- Attend monthly Business After Hours meeting. [$10]
- Attend Chamber of Commerce meeting.
- Attend Rotary.
- Attend Community Arts Partnership board meeting.

JANUARY

Advertising:
Run ad in monthly regional business magazine. [$300]

Publicity:
Do free monthly column for local newspaper on HR trends, issues.

Promotion:
- Sponsor production at Firehouse Theatre. [$1,500]
- Become sponsoring partner of Community Arts Partnership. [$500]

Networking:
- Attend monthly Business After Hours meeting. [$10]
- Attend Chamber of Commerce meeting.
- Attend Rotary.
- Attend Community Arts Partnership board meeting.

FEBRUARY

Advertising:
Run ad in monthly regional business magazine. [$300]

Publicity:
Do free monthly column for local newspaper on HR trends, issues.

Networking:
- Attend monthly Business After Hours meeting. [$10]
- Attend Chamber of Commerce meeting.
- Attend Rotary.
- Attend Community Arts Partnership board meeting.
- Run seminar for local small businesses on human resources trends, issues.

MARCH

Direct marketing:
Send newsletter to clients and prospective clients on HR issues, trends. [$300]

Advertising:
Run ad in monthly regional business magazine. [$300]

Publicity:
Do free monthly column for local newspaper on HR trends, issues.

Networking:
- Attend monthly Business After Hours meeting. [$10]
- Attend Chamber of Commerce meeting.
- Attend Rotary.
- Attend Community Arts Partnership board meeting.
- Attend professional association workshop. [$1,000]

APRIL

Advertising:
Run weekly local newspaper ads for month. [$400]

Publicity:
Do free monthly column for local newspaper on HR trends, issues.

Networking:
- Attend monthly Business After Hours meeting. [$10]
- Attend Chamber of Commerce meeting.
- Attend Rotary.
- Attend Community Arts Partnership board meeting.

MAY

Direct Marketing:
Send letter and information brochure to target client list. [$400]

Advertising:
Run weekly local newspaper ads for month. [$400]

Publicity:
Do free monthly column for local newspaper on HR trends, issues.

Networking:
- Attend monthly Business After Hours meeting. [$10]
- Attend Chamber of Commerce meeting.
- Attend Rotary.
- Attend Community Arts Partnership board meeting.

JUNE

Direct marketing:
- Send newsletter to clients and prospective clients on HR issues, trends. [$300]
- Make follow-up calls to prospective clients sent letter.

Advertising:
Run weekly local newspaper ads for month. [$400]

Publicity:
Do free monthly column for local newspaper on HR trends, issues.

Promotion:
Sponsor team in annual Challenge Industries Golf Tournament. [$350]

Networking:
- Attend monthly Business After Hours meeting. [$10]
- Attend Chamber of Commerce meeting.
- Attend Rotary.
- Attend Community Arts Partnership board meeting.

JULY

Publicity:
Do free monthly column for local newspaper on HR trends, issues.

Networking:
- Attend monthly Business After Hours meeting. [$10]
- Attend Chamber of Commerce meeting.
- Attend Rotary.
- Attend Community Arts Partnership board meeting.

AUGUST

Publicity:
Do free monthly column for local newspaper on HR trends, issues.

Networking:
- Attend monthly Business After Hours meeting. [$10]

- Attend Chamber of Commerce meeting.
- Attend Rotary.
- Attend Community Arts Partnership board meeting.

Total for year—$12,770

You might think that's a lot of money, and a whole lot of time to spend on marketing, and you'd be right. It is a lot of money and it is a lot of time. But remember, some experts advise that as much as 70 percent of your first-year expense budget should be spent on marketing, and as much as 50 percent of your time. This process isn't some theoretical concept. It is the heart of your business and your livelihood, which is bringing in new business. You've got to do it right.

On the other hand, this is the platinum start-up marketing plan. If you don't have the money to spend and can't afford to (or prefer not to) start out accumulating a lot of debt, go for the alternative, bronze plan. Just cut out much of the paid advertising and beef up the direct, personal client contacts and community activities, which are less expensive and possibly even free. Just don't make the mistake of not preparing your marketing plan with as much care, precision, and detail as you do your business plan, because it's just as important to your future success.

LET'S CHECK IN WITH MONICA AND AARON

If you recall, both Monica and Aaron were a little off base in terms of marketing in the early stages of their business planning. But with the help of their respective advisers they both got back on track. And while they each approached marketing somewhat differently, each ended up with what overall was a reasonably effective first-year plan.

Monica didn't have a marketing plan until she met with her SCORE volunteers and they told her in no uncertain terms that she needed one covering every month of the year in a variety of ways. Monica decided her best bet, at least for the first year when clients—and revenue—would be scarce, was to invest in marketing time and effort rather than dollars. In fact, the only paid advertising she purchased was a listing in the Yellow Pages. Her only additional marketing expenses were the cost of printing and mailing business cards, brochures, and letters to prospective clients.

The rest of her marketing campaign was cost free. She volunteered to write a column on human resources issues for the business pages of the local newspaper; she started attending Business After Hours meetings of the local business community; she joined the Chamber of Commerce; she volunteered for the board of the local branch of the American Cancer Society and the local symphony.

Better yet, she followed up her mailings to her growing list of prospective clients with personal calls and get-acquainted meetings in their offices or a local coffee shop. To get through the door, in the case of those who didn't know her name or immediately foresee a need for her services, she promised—and kept her promise—that she would take just ten minutes of their time. That promise alone and her ability to keep it got her a client or two.

Aaron had prepared his marketing plan early on, and didn't do a bad job of it, but his mentor had advised him not to rely so heavily on expensive newspaper advertising. Aaron had planned to run a small ad in the business section of the local newspaper one day a week, every other week throughout the year, and daily the first two weeks after his initial launch. He cut that back to three days a week the first two weeks and once a month thereafter. In addition, though, he bought a separate, small, boxed ad in the Yellow Pages, rather than just a simple listing.

Aaron, like Monica, focused a lot of his marketing plan on less costly strategies: networking at Business After Hours events, doing mailings of his brochure, and teaching a course at the local community college. He also started building his name and reputation by joining as many community organizations and events as he could find time for. But he also made sure that his marketing plan included a good mix of marketing opportunities each month.

MARKETING IS JUST THE BEGINNING

Marketing is all about getting clients. Once you've got them, you must be able to deal with them and make it a win-win situation. That can be tricky. But in Chapter 7 I'll give you strategies for dealing with clients—even with pesky, problem clients—so read on.

7

DEALING WITH THE CLIENT

While your first contact with a prospective client—whether over the telephone or in person—is important in establishing a favorable impression, the essential contact will be your written proposal. While proposals can take many forms and include a wide variety of information, they must all accomplish three key things:

1. Establish your professional credentials and expertise.
2. Communicate what services you will provide, at what cost, and in what time frame.
3. Set a professional but open business tone and footing for the client-consultant relationship.

"The development of the business proposal is the end point of the new business process, and it will ultimately determine whether you are successful in selling the project," writes Thomas L. Greenbaum in *The Consultant's Manual*. It will also set the stage and parameters for your relationship with the client.

PREPARE A PROPOSAL

The first thing you need to do before tackling the proposal is research the client to determine whether the task you are being asked to accomplish will, in fact, solve the company's problems or address its needs. In other words, does the prospective client have a good idea of what his company needs or do you have to educate the client about those needs? Can you propose a project that will address those needs? Usually a background conversation with the client and his key managers, as well as research in trade and business publications, will provide some answers to those questions.

Make sure you ask the client for his preference in proposals: Does he want a brief outline, a very detailed written proposal, or will a verbal proposal followed by a letter of confirmation suffice? Also, suggest a deadline for completing the proposal and an expiration date. That way you minimize the chance of being left hanging as he shops your proposal around for six months.

While a detailed written proposal obviously takes more time, it also allows you to strut your stuff—show the client exactly what you have to offer and how you can help his company achieve its goals. It gives the prospective client more to ponder in making his decision on whether to hire you. A detailed proposal also offers you some protection should the client begin making unreasonable demands or changing the nature of the assignment. It also allows you to develop more realistic cost projections for the project. By the way, be sure to factor the time you spend on the proposal into the total cost of the project.

Some consultants even use the detailed written proposal as a contract, which both parties sign. Greenbaum suggests a ten-part approach to writing a proposal that can be tweaked to meet the needs of most consulting projects. These are his ten basic parts, which I've interpreted and tweaked a bit:

1. The opening. The opening sentence of the proposal should explain the reason for the proposal and the circumstances that prompted it. For example, it might read, "The purpose of this letter is to provide the Acme Company with a formal proposal outlining how the Powers Agency will provide a complete range of human resource services, including a new salary improvement program, for the company." Then follow with something like, "This proposal is a follow-up to our telephone conversation of April 1, in which you reported that your company does not have a human resources department or a human resources manager."

2. Background. Here you should outline key factual information that was provided in your preliminary briefings with company managers. There is some disagreement among consultants over whether this section should be brief and superficial or long and detailed. That's a decision you should make based on your own preference, what you perceive to be the inclinations of the prospective client, and the nature of the project itself.

Whichever you choose, be sure this section at least demonstrates you're sufficiently familiar with the company and its specific needs with regard to the project to develop a sound consulting proposal, and it ensures that all those in a position to evaluate your proposal understand exactly what information you have been given and what has been requested of you regarding the nature of the project.

3. Objectives of the assignment. This should be a very precise and succinct statement about what you will have accomplished by the end of the project. It should be accurate, measurable, and realistic. If the Acme Company has decided to outsource its human resources department in order to save money and improve services, your objective might be ''to provide a complete range of updated and improved human resource services within a budget of $X a year.''

It's important to be perfectly clear in stating the assignment's objective, so there can be no misunderstanding. Item 4 will further help in that regard.

4. Scope of the engagement. This part of the proposal should list in detail exactly what the consulting project will cover. In the case of the Acme project, you will want to list the exact range of services you will provide, from salary and benefits administration to recruitment and training. If you include such words as *updated* and *improved* in item 3, here you need to list exactly what services will be updated and improved, and how.

For example, it may be that the company's benefits package has not been changed in fifty years, and the mix of benefits may need to be updated to include eye and dental coverage, a day care option, or a cafeteria-style approach to benefits selection.

Or an improved salary program may be needed to enhance the company's recruitment and retention efforts. Whatever the case, this section should outline exactly what areas you will address as a consultant, so there can be no misunderstanding about the successful completion of the project.

5. Approach to the assignment. This section explains exactly how you intend to carry out the project and should include the order in which you will undertake specific tasks to achieve the overall objectives. For example, in your proposal to Acme you might include some of the following steps:

- Interview current employees to determine their benefit needs and preferences.
- Research similar-size companies in similar markets to determine their benefit packages.
- Research salaries and wages in the immediate market, in the industry, and at similar-size companies in the region.

Those are just a few examples. You should outline all the steps you'll take to provide the services you need to provide to achieve the overall project objective.

6. Timing. This section should present as detailed a time line for completion of the project as is feasible, with the ultimate conclusion falling within the client's deadline. It will help to provide fairly specific dates for when individual tasks will be started and completed. This detailed time line will give the client a better understanding of and sense of control over the process. Your willingness to put deadlines on your work will help instill confidence in you as a consultant.

7. Staffing. If you're a one-person operation, this section should point that out. If not, it should spell out who in your organization will be part of the project team and who will be doing what. If you intend to subcontract some ongoing services on behalf of the client, that, too, should be explained here. What you don't want to do is suddenly surprise and unnerve the client by turning up at his door with a clutch of unknown faces carrying briefcases, ready to roam through his corridors. In fact, "no surprises" is a good rule of thumb to use in dealing with clients and prospective clients.

8. Qualifications. This is where you clinch the deal by selling yourself to the client. You have to persuade the client that you are uniquely qualified to complete this project successfully. Describe your personal character and qualifications, the experience you've had prior to starting your consulting firm, and the successful projects you've completed for other firms. If you've got a testimonial, attach it as "Exhibit A."

9. Fees and expenses. In this section detail all the financial aspects of the consulting project, including the total fee for completing the assignment. Include all anticipated additional expenses to be borne by the client, such as travel expenses, express mail charges, long-distance telephone costs, extraordinary research expenses, and the cost of presentation materials. Also include the payment schedule for each part of the assignment. It will save you time and hassles later, and perhaps help preserve the business relationship for future projects, if you are very precise and thorough at the outset in stipulating who will bear which expenses.

10. The close. This isn't just the end of the proposal, this is your final opportunity—at least in the context of the proposal—to sell yourself to the client. Recap briefly how interested you are in this project, how committed you are to ensuring the success of each assignment you undertake, and why you are uniquely qualified to ensure its successful completion. Don't relist all of your qualifications, just summarize the key points in a single sentence.

Be sure to encourage the client to contact you immediately if he has any questions or if he needs additional information before making a decision or presenting it to his associates. Then include a couple of sentences informing the client of when and how you will follow up on your proposal. The client should know exactly what to expect from you, and when. This will ensure that when you do call it will be expected, and not perceived as harassment or insecurity on your part.

Finally, a simple signature should follow.

As I noted earlier, your relationship with a prospective client begins even before you present him with your proposal—with the initial contact. But once your proposal is in, it's time to think about building a solid relationship with the client—one that will carry you nicely not only through the life of the current project, but one that will extend to future projects as well.

BUILD A SOLID CONSULTANT-CLIENT RELATIONSHIP

For the freelance management consultant, it's not an exaggeration to say you are the business. That's because what you're selling clients is in your head. Your product is your knowledge and experience, the professional know-how you've accumulated over the years.

When you are the business, the relationship you share with your client is of supreme importance. And that relationship must be grounded on mutual trust and respect. If a prospective client hires you, you've already earned a measure of his respect and trust. In order to complete the project successfully, it's important the client continues to trust and respect you and your professional decisions. If the client is constantly second-guessing you and questioning your judgment, you'll not only get frustrated, you may never be able to complete the job to his satisfaction.

It's also very difficult, if not impossible, to complete a project for someone for whom you have little or no respect and trust. You probably won't find yourself in such an uncomfortable position, but it can happen, so be prepared. Here are some tips that can help you avoid potentially compromising or untenable working relationships:

• Be sure the project involves a problem you can solve—that it isn't a make-work assignment designed to set you or someone else up as a scapegoat or to enhance someone else's corporate position.

• Be sure you know what you need from the project and what you can expect to get from it. Turn the project down if your needs won't be met.

• If you turn a project down because it's not a good match, be sure to do so in a positive, professional way. You want the prospective client to feel comfortable and enthusiastic about considering you for future projects.

• You must genuinely care about your client and his project; if you can't, turn it down.

• Communicate with your client, and make sure he is communicating honestly with you. Don't assume anything; ask, and make sure you get an honest answer.

• By the same token, be sensitive, observant, and intuitive. As a consultant, you sometimes need to read between the lines to avoid corporate politics and other pitfalls.

• If you encounter problems in the project, deal with them immediately and forthrightly. Don't hope they'll go away or the client won't notice something's amiss. If the problem is, in some way, the client, confront him with authority, but not in an accusatory way. Be sure to leave each of you a gracious way to conclude the discussion.

• Never, ever, promise more than you can deliver.

If you keep this advice in mind you should be able to avoid or deal with your most serious problems with clients. But don't let your business relationship rest on whim or even promises. Be sure you have a signed contract, with an escape clause, to formalize your client relationship and your client's expectations. And for your own protection.

BE SURE YOU HAVE A SIGNED AGREEMENT

You'll find that most consultants use business contracts. And since it's just smart business practice, your client isn't likely to object. If she does, chances are good she's a problem waiting to happen, so turn the deal down, fast.

The purpose of the contract is simple: to spell out for all parties exactly what services the consultant is providing, at what cost, what expenses are included and what the time frame or deadline is for completion of the project. Don't forget the escape clause for yourself, but don't be surprised if your client demands one as well. It's all part of the negotiating process involved in any business deal. (I'll write more about the art of compromise and negotiation later in this chapter.)

You can draft a simple, boilerplate business agreement yourself, but it's a good idea to consult your attorney before you sign anything.

Another option is to use the proposal itself as a contract. All you need to do is put an acceptance form at the end of the proposal, and include a place for both parties to sign. When the proposal comes back from the client signed, you're ready to go.

Often, of course, there may be some negotiation over the specifics of the proposal. If you decide to use the proposal as your contract, any changes can be added in the margins and initialed by both parties. Or, you can revise the proposal and have both parties sign the revised copy.

A third option is to use a letter of confirmation. Many people feel a letter of confirmation provides sufficient protection without threatening the consultant-client relationship the way a detailed contract or signed proposal might.

Still, I feel a contract or signed proposal is the way to go. This is a business proposition you are entering into, and any reputable businessperson signs contracts regularly. Just because you are a consultant rather than a vendor or customer should have no bearing on the situation. If it does, perhaps you should reconsider whether you want to accept the assignment. The client is showing signs of being unwilling or unable to treat you as a professional businessperson. That spells trouble for the consultant-client relationship. You may still be able to handle the relationship well, with the proper negotiating skills. But first you have to decide whether it's worth the effort. If it is, read further.

AVOID CLIENT PROBLEMS

One of the reasons you started your own business was to escape the clutches of a whimsical, irrational, or despotic boss, right?

You wanted to be master of your own fate, in control of your work life and schedule, remember? Well, all of that may well be true, but in the reality of your day-to-day work life, even as an independent consultant working for yourself, you may not be able to escape a troublesome, irrational, manipulative relationship with someone on whom you are somewhat dependent: your client.

Clients, like bosses, can make incredible, untenable, even unethical demands on you. Some clients have secret agendas they cleverly conceal from you, from interoffice politics to empire building to attempts at discrediting competitors. Sometimes consultants are given make-work assignments to placate higher-ups. Or they're told to conduct team-building or training sessions that are doomed to failure.

It's best not to get involved in situations like these, in which there's no reasonable chance for success. But how do you know when you're being preprogrammed for failure? It's not easy, but there are signs to look for in your early discussions with prospective clients, and even some you may encounter when you've committed to and started on the project. If you catch a glimpse of any of these, you may need to turn and walk away, fast, and not look back. In some cases it's true that no deal is better than a bad deal. In other cases, when you're already committed, you may have to come up with strategies to deal with the situation.

Here are some warning signs that shout "caution" to any consultant:

- The client wants you to fix something without specifying exactly what needs to be fixed and without giving you his firm commitment and partnership in the effort.
- The client is unable to make a decision on suggested solutions and vacillates between action and no action.
- The client's expectations are unrealistic and/or change repeatedly.
- The client wants you to suggest solutions—to pick your brain—before hiring you for the project.
- The client starts to whittle down the project, and the budget.
- The client suddenly begins to second-guess your ideas and brings new players into the discussions.

Obviously, you need to make a good-faith effort to salvage the relationship and the project. Remember, no two organizations are alike, so every organizational problem is unique. Many organizations, even those that come to you seeking help, are reluctant to make the significant changes needed. As a consultant, you need to be somewhat flexible when you encounter client problems and problem clients. And you sometimes need to be willing to make small differences rather than sweeping changes.

In addition to managing your own expectations and behavior, here are some tips for avoiding problems with clients:

1. Define success for both yourself and your client before you agree to accept the project, and before you sign a contract.

2. Define exactly where the client is now, and make sure that it is understood as the starting point for change in the scope of the project.

3. Don't take your success or the situation personally; this is a business deal, nothing more, and business deals often involve hidden agendas that have nothing to do with you.

4. Discuss problems calmly and professionally with the client. If the client refuses to budge, either walk away or work within the newly understood parameters of the assignment.

5. Don't tackle all the problems, or the whole problem, at once. Try dealing with the situation a little piece at a time, just enough to let you proceed and not enough to alarm your client. This will give your client time to learn to trust your judgment.

Sure, the client hired you because of your professional skills, reputation, and expertise. But that doesn't mean it's easy for her to relinquish her control to you, an outsider. If you're dealing with an entrepreneur—just like you—chances are you're dealing with someone as stubborn, independent, determined, and confident as you. That's not an easy person to persuade, even if she's paying you a lot of money to do just that.

So, in addition to all the steps and tips I suggested above, you better be sure you've mastered the art of compromise.

MASTER THE ART OF COMPROMISE

Whether you've been in the business world three years or three months, you're probably aware that in order to survive you need to learn the art of compromise. If you've managed to survive as an experienced professional in the workplace you've been practicing the art of compromise with some degree of success.

But despite the cliché, practice doesn't necessarily make perfect. And now that you've decided to start your own consulting business, where your relationship with your client is critically important to your business success, you really need to become a master in the art of compromise and negotiation.

Let's face it. When a client contracts with you for a project he has specific needs in mind, some explicit, some implicit. Maybe not even he realizes some of those goals and expectations. That's why you need a written contract, with the client's expectations spelled out. But what that means is there are two of you, one on either side of desk.

That division made by the desk indicates that while you're in theory working together, toward the same goal, you also represent two potentially opposing views on how to meet the goals and expectations. The client may think he knows best, but in reality he doesn't always know best, even about his own company. That may be why he hired you in the first place. So you need to compromise.

But, you can't compromise your professional standards or proceed in a way that compromises the successful completion of the project. That means to achieve a sound and workable compromise—to clinch the deal and keep the project on track—you must negotiate. In addition to negotiating disagreements with your clients, you'll also need to negotiate the terms of your contract and your fee. A good negotiating style will be essential to you in many aspects of your new business.

Negotiate two wins

I'll give you some tips on how to negotiate successfully, so you can achieve the compromises necessary to keep your business relationships afloat. But you can look at these negotiating tips as a sort of bonus, too. While they're designed to help you master the art of compromise your business relationships require, you can use them in your related professional and personal lives as well.

If, as someone once said, "life is a series of negotiations," these tips can help you negotiate your way to a more satisfying life. Remember, the result of a negotiation will be a compromise of sorts, and that means both parties to the negotiation need to feel they've won something. You know, the old win-win strategy.

Usually in a negotiation the wins don't come out totally even. That is, one party may win bigger this time, the other party may win bigger next time. What's important is to be sure each party legitimately can lay claim to a measure of "win." You absolutely want to avoid the disaster a win-lose result can bring to your business relationship.

So what does it take to be a good negotiator? Good negotiators are proactive; they don't accept the status quo without trying to make it better. They actively try to change situations for the better and go after what they want in life and in business. Keep in mind, though, the best negotiators do that while finding a way to make their opposite feel good about the result.

So you negotiate to get what you want in life and in business— to get a better deal or achieve a specific goal. But some people are reluctant to negotiate because they fear they might lose. In other words, if you risk trying to win a negotiation and fail, that means you lose, right? Wrong. First, I repeat: Good negotiators try to end with a win-win situation, not win-lose. Second, failure to win a negotiation doesn't necessarily mean you actually lose something. In most cases, if you're unsuccessful in a negotiation you probably just have to accept the status quo. Or, in a win-win situation, both parties accept less than they wanted but gain something better than the status quo.

How to become a good negotiator

To become a good negotiator you need to change the way you think about negotiating. Most people think of negotiating as a formal process, usually involving a business deal, where opponents sit down on opposite sides of a big boardroom table to resolve weighty matters. And if they think of themselves as negotiating at all, it's in terms of major, formal life events such as buying a house or a car. And then it becomes such a big deal, so to speak, they get strung out about it.

You may not think of yourself as a negotiator, but think again. Don't you resolve small issues every day through conversation? Something like this?

Jacquie: "Can you stop at the market on the way home from work and pick up milk? I have a meeting and will be running late."

Mike: "Okay, but will you call the plumber to fix the garbage disposal and make an appointment for the dog at the vet?"

Jacquie: "Sure, I can do that."

Sound familiar? Sure it does. That's negotiation and compromise, even though we generally don't think about it that way. There's no big mystery to it. Negotiating really is just going after what you want. And that usually means asking for more than the other person wants to give. You need to be willing to ask for more to be a good negotiator. You also need to know what you want, and what the other party is likely to want. That way you can figure out how to end with a deal—a compromise—that leaves both of you feeling satisfied.

Three rules to good negotiating

There are three basic rules for success in negotiating:

1. Know yourself. It's most important to know what result you want to achieve through negotiation. In other words, what you want. Ask yourself, too, if it's worth your time and if it's important to you. Be sure to set a specific goal to work toward. That way, as part of the negotiation, you can be prepared to make concessions in other areas less important to your goal.

But it's also important to know how you tend to respond in certain situations, what makes you crazy, what makes you lose focus, and when you're most awake and sharpest.

For example, are you sluggish in the morning and hit your stride about 4 P.M.? Do your negotiating at that time, if at all possible. Does whining send you into a frenzy that destroys your best efforts at self-control? If you're aware of that you can guard against it.

If you're fully aware of your own personality traits and responses you're going to be better able to negotiate, no matter who your opponent is and his or her own style. But if you're perceptive and observant about people, you should be able to predict what that style will be. Which leads us to Rule #2.

2. Know your opponent. This isn't always easy, but it also isn't quite what it appears at first glance. It helps to be able to read someone's mind or predict exactly how that person will respond in a given situation. But that's not essential. Rather, for the purposes of a negotiation, it means determining if there's a discrepancy of power between you and your opponent. And if your opponent is your client, then of course there's an imbalance of power—he's got more than you do unless you do something about it.

If there's an imbalance of power, you must seek to minimize that imbalance—level the playing field—in order to achieve a successful negotiation. If you fail to even out the perceived balance of power, you run the risk of having such issues as ego and status muddy and even block the negotiation. In fact, you run the risk of failure.

Pollan and Levine, in *The Total Negotiator,* suggest you can better know your opponent and minimize any imbalance of power by answering four questions: What information do I need? With whom should I negotiate? Are there side issues that could cause problems? And, what do I share with my opponent—where can we find common ground?

In the case of a disagreement with your client over how to handle a particular professional issue in your project, there is on the surface an imbalance of power. He's the boss, because he's paying you to perform a service for him. However, you can level the playing field a bit by reminding him that he is paying top dollar for your services precisely because you are an experienced professional and you have had great success in handling similar situations in this manner in the past.

3. Know the situation. This rule is a bit more difficult to follow because each situation is different. In some ways it involves a little bit of both rules 1 and 2. You need to put what you know about yourself and your opponent, and what each of you wants, into the situation. Then figure out what elements of the situation have an impact on your goals and those of your opponent. From there it's just a question of finding the best path to a win-win conclusion. And the best way to get better at all this? That's not rocket science: experience.

There is no right and wrong

Notice that I haven't used the words *right* and *wrong* in discussing negotiation and compromise. That's because they simply don't apply here. There's your position and goal and your client's position and goal. It's irrelevant whether you think your client's goal or tactic is wrong. That's still the point from which he or she is negotiating. The key is to find a way to get what you want while still accommodating your client's needs, at least to the point where you both achieve of measure of satisfaction.

To that end, then, avoid using words like *right* and *wrong* in your negotiations. Be sure to use language that is noncritical and inclusive. Avoid starting all your sentences with "I," and avoid an accusatory tone. This advice might seem basic, but when you're in the heat of battle you'd be surprised at what you find yourself saying and doing.

Body language is important, too. Be open and relaxed. Signal with your body that you're in control of yourself and the situation. Don't bite your nails or tap your feet, or tap on the table with your pencil. That kind of body language signals distress, and can give your opponent some leverage in your negotiation.

Basic tips for successful negotiations

In summary, here are 10 basic tips that will help you achieve successful negotiations, in life as well as in your business relationships:

1. Make your goal specific. That way you're more likely to achieve it.

2. Be sure you understand your opponent's objectives.

3. Don't attempt to negotiate for things that aren't readily negotiable.

4. Decide whether the potential outcome outweighs the time and cost of negotiating.

5. Eliminate or minimize any perceived discrepancies in the balance of power.

6. Negotiate only with someone with the power to make a deal.

7. Prices are invitations to buy, not statements of value.

8. Terms of a deal are as important as dollars.

9. Be sure your body language is relaxed and avoid critical or accusatory language.

10. Aim for a win-win compromise.

The relationship with your clients is at the heart, and central to the finances, of any consulting business. You are your business, and your clients must trust you, like you, and believe in you, in order for you to succeed. Nothing is quite so important to your future as your clients and their success.

But there are other important issues you have to consider in order to ensure your business success. Every detail of your business, no matter how seemingly insignificant, is critical to your success. In your consulting business, you need to become a perfectionist of sorts; or at least attend to details. Everything from your image and grooming to your accounting system and cash flow can affect your success.

MONICA AND AARON

Both Monica and Aaron had an advantage over many new entrepreneurs in their ability to deal with clients and their ability to negotiate and compromise. But even so, the path wasn't always smooth for either of them.

Monica was used to negotiating. Part of her former job had been to serve on the management team that negotiated with the company's union workers. She'd also been advised by her SCORE volunteers to make a written proposal and then be sure she had a written, signed agreement on any job she undertook. They didn't advise her on how detailed that agreement should be, however, and Monica tended to be more trusting than she was wise.

She had no problem with her first client, or even the second, longer-term job for that client. She and the business owner spoke the same language, which was clear, down to earth, and straight-forward. But her third job and second client led to a misunder-standing—or at least that's how she preferred to think of it—that made her change the way she wrote her agreements.

While Monica's written proposal outlined the goals, objectives, and results the client expected—and she agreed to produce—the agreement failed to detail the manner in which those results would be measured. Employee morale was way down and the client wanted her to perform an employee attitude survey and analysis and present recommendations for improving morale.

Monica did the survey and more. She spent hours on site and interviewed people both formally and informally, in their offices but also on the stairs, in the elevator, and in the cafeteria and smoking room. What she found was that the main reason for the morale problem was inadequate compensation, antiquated benefits, and even worse, little recognition for superior performance.

She recommended an overhaul of the compensation and benefits program that could be paid for within five years by increased productivity and a pared down work force. She also recommended a plan not only to reward superior performance but to reinstitute some company social events to foster team spirit and camaraderie that had been dropped to cut costs over the years.

Monica's report and recommendations were not what the client had in mind when he signed her on. He didn't mind the idea of throwing a picnic or Christmas party for the staff, but he didn't want to hear that he wasn't paying his employees adequately. And what he'd actually expected to be told—wanted to be told—was that a small group of middle managers were mistreating the staff and fostering dissension in the ranks.

He told Monica to go back and find out what was really going on. She told him she'd done that, and her report represented the facts of the situation. They were at an impasse, and he said he wasn't about to pay the two-thirds he owed of her fee or her expenses because she hadn't achieved the results he'd contracted for.

It took two months of negotiations and threats of a lawsuit by her lawyer, but Monica finally got paid most, but not all, of what she was owed. The client refused to pay for several hundred dollars' worth of expenses that weren't spelled out in the agreement.

Monica learned her lesson, though. After that she made her written proposal even more detailed than it had been, and used that proposal—with specific detail on how results would be measured—as the basis for her agreements. And she vowed she'd never start any assignment—even for her mother—without a signed agreement.

Aaron's biggest problem initially was with clients who didn't know exactly what they wanted, couldn't make a decision about suggestions he made and options he gave them, and then kept changing their minds halfway through a project. They didn't trust their own judgment, but they didn't trust his expertise either.

He hadn't had quite that kind of experience when he was part of a larger company with a team of professionals around the table with him, backing him up and bolstering the client's sagging confidence. It was a lot more difficult on his own, and something he just had to wrestle with while using not only his negotiating skills but his knowledge of human nature as well.

Besides, he had decided before he ever signed his first client that he wouldn't start on a project until he got 50 percent of his fee up front. That way it would be quite costly for the client to back out in the middle of the project and look for someone else to do the job. So a pep talk, a look at the options, and a reminder that Aaron's time thus far was a costly but sound investment usually did the trick and got the project back on track.

Both Monica and Aaron had learned two keys to success: First, get a very specific, signed agreement that spells out not only goals and expected results but how those results will be measured. And second, get at least 50 percent of your fee up front.

In Chapter 8 we'll tackle some of the financial nuts and bolts, including taxes, accounting systems, and how to ensure prompt payment from slow creditors.

8

FINANCIAL NUTS AND BOLTS

I t's time to think about a budget, what kind of accounting system you should use, what kind of billing system to use, how to get prompt payment from clients, how to insure your business, and how to handle your taxes and a host of other simple but important financial questions. We'll cover all that and more in this chapter, so get out your business notebook and sharpen your pencil. There's still plenty of start-up work to be done.

You provided a first-year financial plan, including estimates of revenues and expenses, in your business plan. Those projections were a good start on a budget, but they were just a start. You need to take those projections a step further and turn them into a real, and realistic, budget from which you can track your revenue and expenditures every month. And then you need to stick to that budget. The cornerstone of every successful business, like the cornerstone of every successfully run household, is a well-planned, well-executed budget.

Your budget should reliably predict all your revenues and expenditures—your cash flow—for a twelve-month period. To do this you need to list all the business expenditures you make regularly or occasionally and compare those with your income. This will help you track how much money you have available at any time and how much you need to meet your business expenses and revenue goals. Your budget will also help you spot problems before they occur, so you can adjust your plans to prevent those and other problems. For example, if you don't land client #2 as quickly

141

as you have projected, you may want to pare down—or beef up—your marketing plan for the next several months.

Keep two things in mind as you prepare your budget: Be complete and honest, and don't underestimate your expenses. Your budget and financial progress will only be as successful as your numbers are real. If you fudge, you're only cheating yourself and your long-term business success.

Your budget shouldn't be just a piece of paper you prepare and then stick in a drawer. To be effective, you need to review your budget and tally your expenditures every day or every week. That way you can see whether your finances are on track, and adjust accordingly.

Your budget is based on three ingredients: revenue (which comes from sales, because that's essentially what you'll be doing), total costs, and profit. If your budget shows you're spending more than you anticipated or earning less, you can adjust immediately by reducing total costs or expenditures, increasing revenues (in other words, expanding sales), or reducing profit expectations.

In the end, of course, the key ingredient for your success, and for the success of any budget you prepare, is sales. You have to sell your services to clients and bring in sufficient revenue to offset expenditures and ensure a profit. A sound budget and good accounting and record keeping can facilitate that process.

GOOD RECORD KEEPING IS CRITICAL

Good record keeping is important for any business. Good records will simplify and facilitate the preparation of your income tax returns. They can also help you keep track of business opportunities; make better, quicker business decisions; and ensure you serve your clients better, with fewer billing problems.

No one, particularly a busy professional, can remember everything he or she needs to know about a client and a project. Good records will help you find important facts quickly and efficiently, and take the guessing out of your work. Finding information quickly and efficiently has always been, and continues to be, a critical factor in the success of any business.

But let's face it, for many creative, ambitious entrepreneurs, record keeping—the administrative side of the business—is just plain *boring*. It's often the last thing you want to think about in planning your new business. Maybe you're thinking, "I can put that off awhile, until I've really got the business going." No way. If you take that approach, by the time April rolls around, or you've got a couple of clients and projects you're immersed in, your desk will be buried in such an avalanche of paper it'll take the ski patrol to dig you out.

Robert B. is a truly creative, professional, public relations consultant who got so consumed by the project part of his business that he neglected the administrative tasks right from the start. In his rational mind he knew better, but subconsciously he felt justified because he wanted to make a big, creative, and impressive splash right from the starter's gun. It didn't take long for that gun to backfire on him.

His billing and record keeping system was so erratic that he'd neglect billing a client for several months, then send a bill one week and another a week later. Sometimes the expenses on the bills overlapped, thoroughly confusing—and annoying—the client. Then, two months after the bill was sorted out and paid, he'd send it all over again because he hadn't recorded the payment properly. Talk about bad client relations.

And to top it off, on several occasions he discovered expense receipts stashed in a pocket of his suitcase or in a bureau drawer, months after the project was completed. The first time he tried to collect payment on the expenses, he ended up feeling so stupid and disorganized—and irritating the client so much—that the next few times he just wrote off the expenses as losses. And the loss wasn't peanuts; it was income he needed at a time he was struggling to get his business going and keep it afloat.

Suffice it to say, that spurred him to rethink his laissez-faire approach to record keeping. "I finally realized good record keeping means good client keeping, and it all adds up to money in the bank," he said.

If record keeping and accounting are truly anathema to you, there are several things you can do. You can hire a good accountant to set up your record keeping system and use her for handling your taxes; you might even be able to trade your consulting services for her accounting service. You can consult a SCORE volun-

teer. Or you could even take a business or accounting course at a
local community college.

I suggest you set aside a specific time each day to update your
records: either first thing in the morning, as soon as you've gone
through your mail, or last thing in the evening before shutting
your office door. Consistency will help keep you on track. Your
record system should be simple to use, easy to understand, accurate, reliable, consistent, and most of all, timely.

Your records should tell you at a glance how much cash you
owe, how much cash is owed to you, and how much cash you
have on hand. They should also include information on:

- Overall profitability
- Monthly income totals
- Accounts receivable totals
- Business operating expenses
- Client information, including your best clients and delin-
  quent clients
- Debts coming due
- Current income sources
- Services most in demand
- Amount invested in supplies and equipment
- Total value of your assets
- Amount of income tax due

This information is necessary not only for preparation of your
taxes, but also for the proper management of your business.

Several software systems are available that provide simple business records required by all businesses; some even have been modified for consulting businesses. Check your local computer or
office supply store or trade journals for information on specialized
consulting business software.

Single- or double-entry bookkeeping

Your business transactions can be recorded in one of two ways:
either single entry or double entry. Single entry is the simplest,

of course. All you do is make a single entry in your record book
that records what each expense is for or the source of each income.
Thus, each entry is either a plus or minus to the amount of cash
you have on hand. If you pay a bill you record a minus and deduct
that amount from your total cash. If you receive a payment for
services it's a plus, and you add that amount to your total. It
works sort of like a simple home checking account.

The single entry method will work fine as long as you have a
limited number of transactions to record. But as you grow and
add clients or services, you may need to use the more complex
double-entry method to ensure your records are accurate. The double-entry method provides a better system of checks and balances,
as you make two offsetting entries for each transaction that balance
each other out. When you receive a check on an outstanding account it's a debit to cash and a credit to accounts receivable. When
you write a check for supplies it's a debit to supplies and a credit
to cash.

Every transaction you record has two entries, on opposite sides
of the book. The left side is the debit side and the right side is
the credit side. The two sides must always balance each other out;
the debits must equal the credits. It may sound complicated, but
really isn't, and the checks and balances will offer you extra accounting security.

If the two sides of your record book don't balance at the end
of the month, check your math first, then check for inaccurately
recorded numbers or transposed numbers, then check to see if
you've incorrectly recorded a debit as a credit.

The double-entry method can be confusing at first. If you're
interested in trying it, I suggest you have it explained to you in
more detail by your accountant.

Tracking accounts receivables and cash receipts

Your cash receipts journal should provide a simple way for you
to track your flow of income. You need to record the date, source,
and amount of income earned. In addition to providing that basic
information for your operating needs and for the Internal Revenue
Service, the journal can show you which of your services are

most in demand and thus help you in fine-tuning and marketing your business.

An accounts receivable journal is similar to a cash receipts journal, but instead of showing you what income you've collected, it shows what is owed to you. That way you can keep track of overdue bills and quickly spot problem accounts.

ENSURING PROMPT PAYMENT

Speaking of problem accounts, the old "check is in the mail" joke isn't a bit funny for the million or so U.S. professionals who are self-employed. Ensuring prompt payment can be a major migraine for the self-employed. Even the best, most prosperous clients can drag their feet in paying their bills, particularly for their smaller, less established creditors. And for the freelance consultant just getting started, with one or two clients and a minimal financial cushion, payments as much as three or four months late can spell disaster.

According to consulting industry experts, nine out of ten freelance management consults who work alone go out of business within two years, mostly because they didn't get paid for their services in a timely way. Trying to get prompt payment can be like, well, pulling teeth from a grizzly bear. And not as exciting. But here are some steps you can take to minimize the problems:

1. Run a credit check on any prospective client before signing a contract.

2. Require your clients to pay an advance of at least 20 percent of your fee.

3. Be sure your contract states the timing of your payment schedule.

4. Specify that the client arranges and pays directly for all of your travel expenses.

5. Get a vendor number at the outset of the project; many corporate accounts-payable departments require that you have a vendor number before they will issue you a check.

6. Bill clients every two weeks rather than monthly.

7. Be sure your contract includes a late-payment penalty of at least 1½ percent a month for payments thirty-one days overdue.

If a client still delays payment despite the above precautions, meet with the client and discuss the problem. If that fails to get action, quit in the middle of the project or refuse further work from the client.

Martin Applebaum was almost forced to shut down his three-person Indiana consulting business and return to the workplace grind—a move that would have meant the end of his life's dream and the loss of his $100,000 investment—when a client refused to pay the remaining $25,000 he owed him. The client, a midsize insurance firm, had awarded Applebaum a $55,000 contract to produce a series of brochures and training manuals.

But when Applebaum finished the project the client refused to pay the remaining $25,000 owed because one of the firm's executives didn't like the photographs used in the printed materials. In fact, Applebaum later learned, the problem was a hidden agenda and corporate politics at its worst. The executive had wanted a different consultant to get the job—one who'd agreed to hire the executive's daughter to do the photography.

The negotiations dragged on for four months, despite Applebaum's threat that he would sue. Finally, when he was unable to make his office rental payments of $2,600 a month, he let his employees go and started looking for a job. But he was outraged, and his anger gave him the courage to stick to his dream. He took out a home equity loan to tide him over and set up shop—on his own—in his basement.

And he made one change in the way he does business: "Now I demand—and get—50 percent of my fee up front. If a client doesn't trust me enough to do business that way, fine. Then they don't trust me enough for me to do business with them at all."

DON'T FORGET YOUR BUSINESS EXPENSES

While Uncle Sam continues to limit what you can deduct as legitimate business expenses, there are many expenses you still can deduct—provided they are well-documented. You'll want to consult with your accountant about exactly what can be legitimately termed business expenses, but in general the IRS considers as deductible only the expenses that are ''ordinary in your business and necessary for its operation.''

Some of the expenses that may meet these criteria include:

advertising

attorney's fees

accounting services

automobile expenses

business publications

charitable contributions

consultants' fees

credit reports

depreciation

entertainment (50 percent only)

freight charges

insurance

interest

licenses

maintenance

materials

membership fees in professional organizations

messenger service

postage

publicity

rent

safe deposit box

seminars

stationery

supplies

taxes

travel

utilities

Obviously, it's important to separate your business expenses from your personal expenses. If you combine business and vacation on a trip, you can only deduct that portion of the trip devoted to business. And, if your spouse accompanies you on the trip, his or her expenses cannot be deducted unless, of course, he or she serves a real business function.

Home-based business owners can also claim a home office deduction in which you deduct part of your rent or mortgage payment. About 1.6 million home-based business owners claim a home office deduction every year. A house, apartment, mobile home, condominium, or even boat all can qualify for the deduction, according to the IRS. However, in order to qualify, your home office must be

your principal place of business,

a separate and distinguishable space in your home,

regularly and exclusively used for business.

You should consult your accountant for details on how to calculate this deduction, as the rules are rather complicated and strict. Or you can call the IRS at 1-800-829-3676 and ask for Publication 587, "Business Use of Your Home," and Form 8829, "Expenses for Business Use of Your Home." You can also download this information from the IRS website at http://www.irs.ustreas.gov/forms_pubs/index.html.

SOME TIPS ON TAXES AND TAX FORMS

The owner of a small business is in a unique position with regard to taxes: you're both a tax debtor and a tax collector. But if you keep good business records, tax time shouldn't make you tear your hair out—much. The nature of your consulting business, its legal structure, and its location, all determine how much you must pay in taxes.

As a debtor, you're liable for various state, federal, and local taxes, which you must pay out of your business earnings. As an agent, you collect various taxes and pass the funds on to the appropriate government agency. If you have employees, you deduct federal income, social security insurance, and FICA taxes from the wages of your employees. If your state requires sales tax on your consulting services, you collect that from clients and pass it on as well.

Federal taxes

As an entrepreneur you're required to pay federal income tax and self-employment tax. If you have employees, you are also responsible for employment taxes.

Federal law requires that all businesses file an annual income tax return. The form you use depends on the legal structure you've chosen for your business: whether it's a sole proprietorship, a partnership, or a corporation. If you've formed a sole proprietorship, you should report your business income and deductions on Schedule C (Form 1040). Attach this schedule to your individual tax return (Form 1040) and submit them together to the IRS.

If, however, you are a partner in a consulting firm, you should report your income and deductions from the partnership on Schedule K-1 (Form 1065), and file it along with your individual tax return. Each of the partners in the firm must do the same, individually. In addition, the total income and deductions for the partnership must be reported on Form 1065.

If you've formed a corporation, you must report its taxable income on Form 1120. Any income or dividends you receive from the corporation also must be included on your individual tax return.

Self-employment tax

Self-employment tax is similar to the Social Security tax paid by employees. The difference is you pay both the employer's and employee's share yourself, and instead of having it withheld from your paycheck you pay it directly. For additional information on self-employment tax, get IRS publication 533, "Self-Employment Tax."

Federal law requires that sole proprietors and partners pay their income and self-employment taxes each year on a pay-as-you-go basis. Instead of paying them in a lump sum at the end of the year, as most individuals do, you pay them in installments quarterly, on April 15, June 15, September 15, and January 15 of the following year.

You are required to pay a quarter of your total tax bill on each date, but you must ensure that you prepay at least 90 percent of your previous year's tax bill or you may be subject to a penalty.

Tax returns for corporations are due on the fifteenth of the third month following the end of its taxable year, which may or may not coincide with the calendar year.

Employment taxes

If you employ others in your consulting business you most likely will need to pay employment taxes, including:

- Federal income tax, which you must withhold from your employees' wages
- Federal unemployment tax, which you, as the employer, must pay
- Social Security tax, part of which you withhold from your employees' wages and the remainder of which you contribute as the employer

You must report both the income tax and the Social Security tax on Form 941, and pay both taxes when you submit the forms. You report and pay the federal unemployment tax on a different form, Form 940. You can get additional information on employment taxes from IRS publication 15, "Circular E."

State and local taxes

Tax laws vary from state to state and municipality to municipality, so your state and local tax bill will be dependent on your location.

New York and California, for example, have higher state tax rates than most other states.

Some of the taxes imposed at the local and county level include business taxes, licensing fees, and income taxes. Check with your attorney or accountant, or with local government authorities or the Chamber of Commerce, to be sure you are meeting local tax laws.

PROTECT YOURSELF WITH INSURANCE

While operating a home-based consulting business is relatively low risk, it's still a considerable investment that should be protected through business insurance. You'll need special insurance to cover your home-based business, and you should also consider professional liability insurance.

About 60 percent of home-based businesses are uninsured or underinsured, according to a survey by the Independent Insurance Agents of America. While your home most certainly is insured for fire and other damage, you can't rely on your homeowner's insurance to cover your home business. If you check the fine print, you'll probably find that your homeowner's policy specifically excludes business activities.

If business activities are not excluded, they're probably covered only for up to $2,500 for loss of property, such as a computer, if it's on the premises and $250 if the loss is not at home. A homeowner's policy definitely won't cover loss of income if a fire forces you to shut down or temporarily pay rent elsewhere, nor will it provide liability coverage if a client is injured walking up your driveway.

What you need to look for is called an "in-home business policy." Such policies usually cover personal business property, general liability, and loss of income. Consult an insurance agent who specializes in home-based business coverage. The agent will conduct a risk analysis of your property to determine the value of the property, including your equipment and furnishings. Be sure that the policy covers all business-related items for the full cost of each item, not the depreciated value. After all, if you have to replace your equipment you'll have to pay full price.

For more information on how to insure your home-based business, contact The Insurance Information Institute, 110 Williams Street, 24th Floor, New York, NY 10038; 212-669-9206. Ask for their booklet, "How to Insure Your Home Business."

Professional liability insurance

You also should investigate professional liability insurance. Any professional who gives others advice or information, or performs professional services for clients, should seriously consider purchasing professional liability insurance. This coverage will protect you against damage claims a client may make charging you with mistakes that hurt his business or with failure to complete an assignment.

The most common type of professional liability insurance for consultants is "errors and omissions insurance." It doesn't come cheap, that's for sure, but it may be possible to get a deal by going through a professional association to which you belong.

Health insurance

You also, of course, need to insure your own health, now that you're no longer covered by an employer's business insurance. You have numerous options, depending on where you live. Health Maintenance Organizations (HMOs) provide an affordable option, and become quite competitive in the range of preventive and other care they offer. You'll want to check out the quality of the physicians in a particular HMO, and find one with physicians who suit your needs and personality.

You can buy insurance policies with high deductibles, in the $1,000 to $2,000 range, or choose a preferred provider plan, where you pick from a menu of physicians with whom the insurer has existing agreements.

Some insurers offer major medical coverage at reduced rates that automatically kick in if you incur very high medical costs or hospital visits. Such policies may be available through your professional organization, or, if you're over age 50, from the American Association of Retired Persons. The key with health insurance is to shop around and choose your plan carefully, with your own particular needs in mind.

There's no way around it. Health insurance for you and your family is a number one priority and a number one budget concern for your business. So shop around, then bite the bullet up front and find a policy that meets your needs and those of your family members. In the long run it'll be well worth the investment.

MORE ON MONICA AND AARON

To put it simply, Monica lost money because she didn't put her financial house in order right at the start. Okay, she had an excuse—one used by many a novice entrepreneur. She was so focused on getting her business off the ground, in marketing herself, and then in doing an outstanding job for her first several clients that she neglected to set up her accounting and billing system until it was too late.

Because of that she didn't bill her first few clients promptly, and for a time actually threw receipts in her desk drawer, including those for billable expenses she paid out of her own pocket. She figured she'd get to them later, when there was a lull in the business.

That's when she ran into trouble with her second client and ended up eating a stack of billable expenses herself—several hundred dollars' worth. Had she billed the client for those expenses as they arose, biweekly, she wouldn't have been left holding the bag when the project ran into trouble.

That was an ugly wake-up call for Monica. But it was also a blessing in disguise. She'd been telling herself she was just too busy consulting to set up a billing and accounting system. When she ended up losing what she was fairly owed, she finally faced the reason she'd put off getting her record keeping in order, which was that it a task she simply hated to contemplate.

It wasn't that she couldn't do it, just that she considered it drudgery. She solved that problem handily, by hiring an accountant to set up a computerized system that would be simple and easy to use. Not only did she start billing biweekly, she set aside two hours every Monday morning to bring her accounts up to date. She got an unexpected payoff that went beyond dollars and cents: not only was she keeping better track of her finances, the new system also gave her a better overview of her business, including exactly what services she was providing for which clients and what materials and supplies she was using.

Predictably Aaron, with his ultraobsessive dedication to detail, had organized his double-entry bookkeeping system and weekly, not biweekly, billing process before he landed his first client. Aaron made it a practice to end each day by spending a half hour to an hour updating his records and accounts. He felt it helped him finish his business day with a sense of satisfaction—at the very least he knew he'd accomplished those simple mathematical or recording tasks.

Strangely enough, Aaron shunned technology on only this point: he preferred to use the very old-fashioned pencil and hard-bound ledger book his father had used long ago to keep the household accounts. He liked the actual rustle of the paper and the way the smell of the rubber eraser stirred his physical senses. Small things, he said, but they reminded him every day that he was living his entrepreneurial dream.

With these financial nuts and bolts in place it's time to put the finishing touches on your consulting business. In Chapter 9 we'll talk about the ethics and etiquette of consulting, and the importance of image to the professional consultant. These are the fine touches that will help set you and your business apart and start you on the road to success.

9

THE FINISHING TOUCHES

I t's time to put a glossy patina—the finishing touches—on your new business. The finer points of consulting ethics and etiquette, image and impact, might seem like small details, but they're important ones that can make the difference between you and your competitors, between a business that just gets by and one that stands out as a major success story.

It's safe to say that as an entrepreneur, you won't have any detail that relates to your new business's success that is too small to concern yourself with. You might say to yourself, "These details can wait until after I'm in the game, until my new business is up and running." And perhaps they could. But I don't recommend hitting the road to success without a full tank of gas and a spare; why take the chance? Business competition is too keen and too cutthroat for you to start without everything you're going to need to ensure your success.

THE IMPORTANCE OF IMAGE

The word *image* has a number of meanings, several of which it would be useful to note here. According to *Webster's New World Dictionary*, the Second College Edition, the word *image* is defined as, "4a) a mental picture of something; conception; idea; impression; b) the concept of a person, product, institution, etc., held by the general public, often one deliberately created or modified by publicity, advertising, propaganda, etc. 5) a type; typical example;

symbol; embodiment. . . . 6) a vivid representation; graphic description. . . .''

The image you and your business project to the public is critically important to your future success. The good news is that you can shape and control, define and cultivate that image. In fact, everything you do as owner of the business and as its emissary—every detail that comprises the ''vivid representation; graphic description'' of your business, from your business card to your promotional materials to your personal attire—works together to form your business image.

The image you project must, first of all, match the expectations of your clients. But equally important, it must also be compatible with your own personality and style. In other words, you must be genuine and authentic in your cultivation of your professional style and image. Dishonesty is as obvious as body odor and can be just as disastrous to your image.

The professional image that's appropriate and honest for a graphic design consultant, for example, would not be appropriate for a tax consultant. The graphic designer needs to project an image that shouts creativity, excitement, originality, even surprise. It should be clear from just looking at the designer and speaking with her for a few minutes that you're in the presence of a person with artistic skills and an original way of looking at things. The tax consultant, on the other hand, should project an image of conservative stability, sound judgment, trust, and confidence.

Your image is a combination of four things: the way you look, the things you do, what you say, and your environment. If you analyze and alter one or more of those four ingredients, you can alter the whole picture.

The way you look

There is no right and wrong appearance. As I noted earlier, a graphic designer can look trés artistic and flamboyant without raising an eyebrow, while a tax consultant would be wise to look somewhat sober and conservative.

As a home-based consultant, of course, you can look any way you like in your home office, as long as you're sure a client or prospective client isn't likely to appear at your door. But when

you're going to be meeting with clients, you better look professional, successful, and appropriately attired for the part the client
expects you to play. Is that dishonest? Not at all. Everyone wears
a "work face" and a more casual, even sometimes quite different,
"personal face." Everyone needs to be able to let her hair down
at home—oops, make that—off the job.

That doesn't mean you need to wear what amounts to a uniform,
or conform exactly to someone else's idea of what you should
look like. Far from it, in fact. You do want to be noticed, to stand
out as a person of success and good taste, so use your good
judgment to make your own unique statement that spells success.

The things you do

They way you conduct yourself in your dealings with the client
can have a tremendous impact on your relationship. As a seasoned,
skilled professional, you should view yourself, and conduct yourself, as an equal. At the same time, as a good businessperson, you
should always consider the client's needs first.

While your relationship with the client is a business relationship,
you need to treat him warmly and personably; after all, he's a
person as well as a businessman. Don't be presumptuous, but don't
be standoffish, either.

And don't forget to consider the client's needs not just in terms
of the big picture—the various aspects of the assignment—but in
the little details as well. Make sure the client has everything he
needs while he's on your turf. Take his coat, ask if he'd like
coffee or water, or if he needs a note pad or pen.

By thinking of your client's well-being and anticipating his
needs you're giving him a better understanding of not just your
courtesy, but of your overall competency and efficiency.

What you say

The specific words you use in describing yourself, your business, and
your client's needs—even your tone of voice—can enhance or detract
from your professional image. Obviously, you should always speak
to clients with courtesy and respect, even in trying situations.

Use correct terminology for your profession, but don't overuse jargon. Most of all, don't try to oversell or impress the client with long-winded, unnecessary explanations or accounts of your accomplishments. Remember how you always hated a braggart? A simple explanation of what you've done and for whom, when asked, as well as your proposal and printed materials, will accomplish more than a speech.

Don't forget that your printed materials, such as your business card and brochures, also convey your image. They should be professional and striking, but also give a sense, both graphically and subliminally, of what you're all about.

If you can't afford the services of a graphic designer to come up with a professional-looking, appropriate logo designed especially for you, keep it simple and stick to a clean-lined, simple type face and clear, direct language. Forget the logo until you can afford the right one. An unprofessional or inappropriate logo or type can go a long way toward undoing the professional image you are striving for.

Your environment

Your environment, as much as your appearance and your speech, gives subtle hints about the kind of person you are, so keep that in mind as you are furnishing your office space, particularly if you'll be bringing clients to your space rather than meeting them in their domain.

First, be sure your environment is a soothing, subtle background to the image you want to project, not a glaring, obtrusive counterpoint. Unless, of course, you're a designer who needs to proclaim your creativity in every way possible. If you're a trend tracker it would be entirely appropriate to have a futuristic, avante-garde, glass-and-chrome office. If you're a tax consultant, better stick to solid, established, soothing mahogany, leather book–lined shelves that bespeak the wisdom of the ages, and Oriental carpets.

In either case the focus should be on you, not your decor.

A cautionary tale

Harold Webster almost let his personal problems derail his management consulting business. Webster is an environmental consultant who specializes in the area of hazardous waste regulations and management. He started his Texas business, Webster Waste Consulting Services, five years ago at age forty-five, after the manufacturing firm he worked for decided to downsize, leaving him without a job but with his first client.

That client led him to several others, and two years later Webster was pulling in almost more business than he could handle alone, with just some part-time clerical help. In fact, he was thinking of expanding by hiring another consultant. That's about the time the problems started.

Webster's wife of twenty-two years left him for a younger man, one who owned several fitness centers and who specialized, Webster said, on polishing his biceps every hour. Not that Webster was biased, of course. Webster now admits somewhat sheepishly that when he got over the shock and pain he decided he better spruce up, and maybe went a bit overboard.

He went to a hair stylist instead of his old barber and got a new, slicked-back hairdo and bought a couple of new suits—Armani knock-offs—silk shirts, and, okay, even a silver chain. "I thought gold would be too much, but silver seemed kind of conservative. What did I know?"

And he started taking what he thought was subtle notice of the women working in his clients' office, schmoozing instead of reading reports while he waited for appointments with clients. Nothing rude, just more friendly.

The fallout didn't take long. Webster said in a couple of months he noticed a new coolness in his clients. Then, a prospective client he had written a sound proposal for—referred by one of his oldest clients—cut him off without even discussing his proposal. He couldn't figure out the abrupt freeze, so he decided to ask his original client, with whom he still worked.

Webster was lucky, because the client was an honest person and one with whom he had a long working relationship. Even so, it wasn't easy. Basically, Webster said, the client told him he'd changed since his divorce, and professionally speaking, it wasn't for the better. Maybe he was still the same person, with the same expertise, but he looked and acted different.

"'He told me, 'This is hazardous waste we're talking about. We need someone professional, responsible, and most of all, stable. And frankly, you just don't give that impression anymore. You may still be the same person, but you don't appear the same. It's unsettling.'''

It was all a question of image, and Webster cleaned up his act after that frank talk. Last I heard, his business was back on track. Not yet ready to expand, but moving in that direction.

Words of advice about personal style and other matters

There's no question that a professional image is important. But more important, says consultant Nancy Veazey of College Park, Maryland, is finding the perfect business focus for your personal style.

Veazey started her sole proprietor consulting business, TrainingSmith/XtraAssets, in 1994 after leaving a large retailer where she'd worked for ten years. She said she wanted more freedom and fewer constraints "on using my talents and abilities—and to escape from organizational politics." She was also midway through her master's program in human resource development, and wanted to cut out the long commutes and be able to spend more time at home.

She started out "with a kind of generalist training and instructional design focus" as she tried to find the right mix of services to attract clients and keep herself engaged. It was a struggle, but she now says, "I believe my business is just taking off. I certainly went through several false starts. I expect to have the lifestyle I want and get paid well for something I love to do. I'm not looking for too much growth because I would have to sacrifice in terms of quality of life. I'm trying to do high quality work versus quantity; that's not everybody's goal." Still, she expects her business to double in the next year.

What wrought the turnaround? "I think the biggest problem I've faced is finding a focus for my business that suits my personal style and values. *And*, translating that into marketing terms. I used to struggle with how to explain to people exactly what my business was. I wanted to try to do too many things. I'm sure as I go through this year I'll continue to refine my services but I feel I have defined them pretty well at this point."

So what has she come up with? Her business provides "expert

services for other consultants and organizational development practitioners. I do work that allows them to spend more time with their clients: front-end analysis, research, surveys, white papers, draft reports, job descriptions accompanying realignments and organizational changes, and instructional design for new policies or training that grows out of an intervention. The thrust of my business is subcontracting to other training and organizational development professionals.''

Mostly she works for small consulting firms, and she believes subcontracting and consulting teamwork is a trend that's here to stay. ''More and more I see colleagues temporarily banding together for specific projects in order to bring enough talent and resources to bear. I believe this is the wave of the future.''

Veazey has additional advice for those getting started:

• ''Get to know yourself; complete a Myers-Briggs assessment and read up on your style preferences. Understand the dilemmas inherent in consulting for your personality type (taking work to get work versus having the lifestyle you want, etc.) and decide how these dilemmas affect you personally.

• ''Survey other consultants in your field to get a good feel for the real 'going rate.' Don't overprice or undervalue your work. Be flexible and quote ranges, but don't work for free, unless you're selectively marketing yourself through some pro bono work.

• ''Recognize your need to bounce ideas off others or have some professional interaction: join a professional association, start a support group, keep in contact with others through phone and E-mail.

• ''Educate yourself about the perils and joys of telecommuting if that's what you plan to do. You may need more structure than this arrangement provides.''

NOURISHING CREATIVITY

Every consultant has to be creative. After all, you're in the business of solving problems, and that often involves coming up with new ideas.

Webster's defines creativity as "artistic or intellectual inventiveness."

Creativity means thinking new thoughts, having new ideas, going beyond the known to the unknown and transforming it. Being inventive, in other words. To be successful as a consultant and as an entrepreneur, you'll need creativity to find just the right focus for your business, to find the right clients, and then to solve their problems and keep them.

To remain competitive in the marketplace, you need to nourish your creativity and be able to tap into it regularly. Easier said than done, right? Not necessarily. Hal Lancaster, in his September 16, 1997, *Wall Street Journal* column, "Managing Your Career," noted that creative people have some qualities in common, including "keen powers of observation, a restless curiosity, the ability to identify issues others miss, a talent for generating a large number of ideas, persistent questioning of the norm and a knack for seeing established structures in new ways."

Better yet, Lancaster has some suggestions for developing those qualities yourself. He suggests you build a tolerance for bad ideas, think big, seek out diverse friends, and discipline your creative urges. I agree. Here's my own take on Lancaster's tips:

Build a tolerance for bad ideas. The only way to be creative and encourage creativity is to promote an environment in which people—you included—don't feel they put themselves at risk or make themselves ridiculous if they come up with a bad idea on occasion.

People who are truly creative seem to be a fountain of ideas, bubbling up continuously. And not all of those ideas are ones they will act on—good ones. But if they felt those bad ideas were going to be laughed at, the fountain of creativity would soon dry up.

So encourage creativity by letting your own ideas and those of others flow freely, without fear of ridicule. The heavier your flow of ideas, the better your chances are of coming up with some good, creative ones that will serve you well.

Think big. Thinking big involves looking beyond the short term to the long term. It also means dreaming dreams and turning them into reality, being willing and ready to accept the impossible as possible—and doable. Think beyond the narrow parameters of a problem; don't let someone else's definition of the problem limit your understanding of it or your ideas for solving it. Creativity comes from opening up the box, not closing it.

Seek out diverse friends. Different people, with different interests, experiences, and approaches to life have different ways of thinking, analyzing, and solving problems. You can learn much by seeking out people who are different from you in one way or another, by talking with them, spending time with them, and being sensitive to their differences. It's another way of opening up doors in your mind and letting new ideas flow through.

Creativity isn't something you can put on your schedule to recharge once a week. It also isn't the property of a select few. Creativity should be something you nourish all the time, as a regular, valued part of your personality, experience, and professional life. Seek new experiences, new ideas, new ways of thinking and analyzing problems. If you keep an open mind and flexible way of thinking, you'll find your creative juices simply don't dry up.

THE ETHICS AND ETIQUETTE OF CONSULTING

As a professional consultant hired to give expert advice that can affect the future of your client's business, you hold a unique position of trust with your client. Remember, you are your business, and in every dealing you have with your client it's your reputation, ethics, and moral standards that are on the line, in addition to your professional expertise.

So what's the big deal? Of course you always put your client's interests first and do the right thing, right? You're a trustworthy, moral, and ethical person, so there shouldn't be a problem. But sometimes issues get muddy and "the right thing" isn't always clear. Sometimes, in fact, it's clear as mud.

What if you learn some information in confidence that can affect your client's business? What if you feel your client's interests are not in the best interests of another client, or of society in general? What if you can benefit personally from a recommendation you make to a client? These are all situations that aren't cut and dried, in which you have to make ethical, even moral decisions in determining how you will act.

As a consultant, some of the situations and issues you'll be dealing with that are likely to lead to ethical dilemmas are the following:

personal relationships
payment
performance
promotion tactics
professional standards
confidentiality
conflict of interest
insider information
loyalty
objectivity
qualifications
quality control

Personal relationships

Several kinds of personal relationships on the job can lead to moral and ethical dilemmas. First no-no, of course, is to mix business and romance. But you can't always control where your heart leads you or when. Even more impossible to control is the behavior of those you work with.

Your best bet in both situations is usually honesty. Let your client know of any relationship you develop that may have the potential to affect your behavior on the job, and discuss the best way of dealing with this complication.

If there's a personal relationship between people with whom you must work in carrying out your client's assignment—and that potentially could affect the project—you have to decide whether to discuss it with them, with the client, with both, or just ignore it.

I don't recommend ignoring it, but there's no one-answer-fits-all-situations solution. Follow your gut and your personal standards, and be sure your professional image doesn't get compromised in the process.

Payment

You deserve to be paid appropriately for your work as a consultant. By the same token, your client has a right to know in advance how much he can expect to pay for your services and expenses and to receive detailed, itemized accountings of your billable hours and expenses.

In order to avoid problems, you need to have a written agreement that includes your fees and expenses as well as a payment schedule. And, most important, you need to keep detailed, accurate records from which you bill. If you're going to avoid payment problems and billing questions you can't use the throw the receipt in the shoe box and dig it out later approach to record keeping. Your records should be so logically and clearly organized and maintained that if your client chooses, he can look at the books, electronic or otherwise, and clearly see the justification for his bills.

No matter how accurate and organized your records, you'll most likely encounter other ethical questions relating to payment. For example, what is a reasonable expense versus an excessive one? How do you charge for an expense if it applies to several clients? When should an expense be considered overhead and when should it be charged to a client? And, if a project expands beyond the original parameters and estimates, who should foot the bill? Should you eat the cost, or should you try to renegotiate the contract so your client shares some or all of the cost?

Again, there are no easy, cut-and-dried answers. In most cases use the "reasonable" approach. What seems most fair and logical? Maybe bill clients on a prorated basis for a share of the expense that all benefit from. Suggest renegotiating an expanded project if the increased scope is primarily caused by client demands. But if the client appears truly offended, smile, bite the bullet, demonstrate your honesty and integrity, and build a better relationship for the future. The loss of profit now will probably reap bigger rewards in the future.

Performance

When you contract with a client to provide a specific service or solve a problem, you are in effect guaranteeing that your company is able to meet the terms of the contract and provide the service. That's a matter of trust, reputation, and of course, contractual obligation. So in terms of ethics, be sure you know what you're capable of and don't promise more than you can provide.

But there's potentially a further ethical question involved in performance: who will be doing the actual performing for the contract in question? In many cases the client assumes that when dealing with a freelance consultant, or a small consulting firm, the person he is negotiating with—you—are the person who will be doing the work. It's your expertise he is hiring.

So if there's a chance you may subcontract parts of the assignment, or employ the talents of a junior member of your team, you have an ethical obligation to make that clear to your client up front.

Promotion tactics

The key ethical concern in promotion is the sometimes fine line between honestly promoting services you are capable of providing by boasting of the quality and expertise of those services, and downright lying. All advertising and promotion involves some embellishment, some flattering spotlighting of your finer qualities and skills. The goal of promotion is, after all, to make yourself and your business as alluring to prospective clients as possible. To sell.

By the same token, however, it's unethical to promote your business with false or misleading information and claims. Again, you can't lie about what services you can—and cannot—provide.

Put ethics aside for a moment in favor of image. Some consultants have gone the way of banks and supermarkets and newspapers in terms of marketing, offering everything from free cell phones to free computer software as signing bonuses to new clients. Hey, it's your business, and even some attorneys are trying the hard sell, using shouting TV shill men to boost sagging sales.

I don't advise throwing toasters at prospective clients. You're a professional, and your professional image is more important than the odd client or two who might be attracted by a free pager or set of carving knives. So make sure your promotion methods match not only your ethical standards but your image as well.

Professional standards

Professional standards can become a slippery, two-way street in the middle of a consultant-client relationship. For the consultant, the question of which way to negotiate that slippery street can become an ethical dilemma. Your client no doubt has hired you based, at least in part, on the professional standards and accomplishments you demonstrated during interviews and in your written proposals. You've pointed with pride to other satisfied clients and successful assignment outcomes. You're proud of your work, and it's the excellence of your work that drew the client.

But in the middle of the project several things might occur: the client could begin to feel the need to pinch pennies and start to pull back financially from the project, or a hidden agenda might begin to take shape that culminates in the client asking you to compromise your standards.

Maybe all along the client pretended to buy into the whole package you're recommending, knowing full well he'd only pay for and implement bits and pieces. That could seriously compromise its success, and at the very least, jeopardize quality control. It's a question of professional standards all right—yours and the client's.

As much as possible, it's smart business to satisfy any doubts you may have on this issue at the outset. Otherwise you're left between a rock and a hard place: pulling out of the project and losing money or settling for less than your professional standards dictate.

It's not a question you can answer now, not knowing the full context of whatever situation might occur, but be prepared—it's bound to happen someday. And the best way to avoid it as long as possible is with honest conversation with the client in advance, and careful language in your contract.

Confidentiality

As a management consultant you're in the business of information. Clients, in fact, pay you for information. They also pay you to keep your information, which becomes their information, to yourself. So if you can't keep a secret, you're in the wrong business. Confidentiality is of the utmost importance and is a key component of the consultant-client relationship.

In fact, the ultimate success of the client's business may be in your hands, depending on the nature of the confidential business information to which you have access. So handle your client's business information in the same way you handle your own—with zipped lips.

On the other hand, you may inadvertently come across information that compromises or threatens your client. You have to decide how to deal with such information. For example, what if you learn that the client is rushing to market with a product that still has "bugs" and is potentially dangerous? Or what if you learn the client has landed an important government contract by making illegal payments to the company's officers?

In these cases you must think carefully about your obligation to your client, but also about your obligation to yourself and to your own reputation and standards. And last but not least, consider the public welfare and public trust. Then do what's right. You may not like doing it, but you'll usually know what's the right course of action.

Conflict of interest

Some of these ethical issues begin to overlap, and this is one. Confidentiality and conflict of interest often are likely to overlap. You learn something from one client that can help or hurt the business of another client. Do you maintain confidentiality or put yourself into a potential conflict of interest situation by telling what you know?

Then there are your interests and those of society, both of which your current client may also be jeopardizing. Whose interests come first? That's a question you must answer knowing all the facts of the case; but generally speaking, the interests of your current client should come first. The conflict arises if those interests clash with the greater good. That's not always easy to sort out.

One thing you can try to do is limit your assignments with different clients to areas in which it appears likely there will be no conflict. That's sometimes easier said than done, but it's worth a try.

If you're in the middle of two assignments for different clients and realize there's a conflict, the most important thing to do is to immediately let your clients know what's happened and to negotiate a solution that brings a "win" and peace of mind to each of you. If one client refuses to discuss any compromise solution, it may be best to terminate the contract—and put your reasons in writing.

One other thing to remember: Never, ever, steal a good employee from your client. That would be a real conflict of interest and would cast a huge shadow over your trustworthiness in all areas. If a client's employee comes to you expressing interest in making a change and coming to work for you, tell him you can't possibly participate in such a discussion while you are working with his employer and hoping to continue bidding on assignments from the company in the future. And don't be coy, hinting that as soon as the contract ends you'll be eager to entertain such a discussion. Make it clear it's an issue of loyalty and conflict of interest and it doesn't meet your ethical standards.

Stealing employees is as tacky and unethical as stealing ashtrays—and trade secrets.

Insider information

The use of insider information—that is, information about a company that is not known to the general public—is unethical, and often illegal. It is unethical for a consultant to use her "insider" knowledge of a company to gain, financially or otherwise, from that knowledge.

If it's a question of using special information about a company to make a decision to buy shares in the company—before the information becomes public—it's illegal. However, if by working for the client you've gained insight into company operations, values, and goals and feel the company is a good bet for future financial gains, it's neither illegal nor unethical to buy stock in the company.

As long as your decision is based on your own personal evaluation and analysis, and not on any special insider information, you're on safe and acceptable ground. However, to avoid even the appearance of impropriety, many consultants make it a rule never to buy stock in companies for which they consult.

Not all cases of insider information involve purchase of company stock. Other situations involving insider information might occur if you, as a consultant, know the client intends to build a satellite operation at a suburban location and you buy real estate or a convenience store in the area. Or if you share that information with someone who capitalizes on it. Depending on the situation it may seem like just a matter of good business sense, but be careful. If it involves disclosure of confidential information, it's at least unethical.

Loyalty

The question of loyalty should be a simple one, but don't always count on that. Obviously, as a consultant your loyalty is with your client, right? Right. But exactly who is the client? Usually the client is the corporate name written on your business agreement. But that's often just a corporate entity, not a real person.

What about the person who signs on the dotted line for the company and with whom you deal regularly, the CEO or president? Or maybe he's not your operating contact; maybe you work in partnership with someone lower in rank. And then there's possibly a board of directors to complicate matters further.

If you find mismanagement, misconduct, or illegal activity, where does your loyalty lie and where should you go? That's not always easy to sort out, but let your ethics, morals, and professional standards guide your way.

Objectivity

In addition to the other reasons I've cited, such as your professional expertise and reputation, your client has hired you in order to bring your objective eye to his business situation. Presumably, you'll be able to see the situation more objectively, with less bias, than those inside the company who are more directly involved.

Therefore, if for some reason you lose your ability to be objective, whether because of a personal relationship that develops or a special product or service you offer, you have a moral obligation to inform the client of your loss of objectivity. It may be a situation you can discuss, resolve, or work around. But that should be his call, not yours, when he's been given all the facts.

Qualifications

You have a moral and ethical obligation to take on only those assignments that you have the skills and expertise to complete to the client's satisfaction. That doesn't ensure that you will or must complete the assignment to the client's satisfaction, only that you can.

It's natural to continually seek to expand your skills and stretch your talents. Most entrepreneurs have a habit of seeking new and great challenges; that's what makes them good entrepreneurs. However, in doing so be sure it's a stretch that's reasonable for the skills and expertise you do have, and don't overstate your skills or mislead the client about your experience and expertise.

Again, it's a fine line, but one you need to be aware of continually. You'll be gaining skills and expertise in new areas with each assignment you undertake, so that means you should regularly analyze your skill set and the services you offer, so you neither sell yourself short with an outdated résumé nor mislead prospective clients about talents.

Quality control

Again, this is where your professional reputation and standards are on the line. It's your job to complete the assignment with the proper quality controls in effect to ensure that the project is not compromised in any way. If the client begins to eat away at the project costs, taking shortcuts, using inferior products, or in any way potentially jeopardizing the integrity of the project, you need to speak up.

If you aren't able to persuade the client to put the project back on track, or to come to some agreement that achieves less than you'd hoped but doesn't totally compromise your professional standards, think about signing off and cutting your losses.

Remember, your business is only as good as your ethics, standards, and reputation.

Develop a personal code of ethics

Many consultants decide at some point to develop their own personal ethics code, one that they may share with prospective clients. This in no way guarantees that ethical conundrums won't occur, but it can certainly put a client on notice about your ethical and professional intentions.

In addition, a personal ethics code is something you can refer to when you suddenly find yourself in the middle of an ethical muddle that makes it hard to see the forest for the trees. It's always handy to refer to guidelines, rather than to start afresh every time you have a crisis. And, if you take the time and trouble to develop an effective, workable code of ethics it can help shape the way you do business and build your practice throughout your career.

A good place to start if you decide to go this route is with the codes developed by professional organizations. The American Society for Training and Development (ASTP), the Association of Consulting Management Engineers (ACME), and the Institute of Management Consultants (IMP) all have detailed codes of ethics that members are expected to adhere to. Obviously, you'll want to personalize your code and make it fit your unique business, but these offer a good starting point.

All codes of ethics, no matter what your particular consulting field, should refer to:

- Upholding professional standards
- Obeying the laws
- Protecting the client's interests
- Contracting only for those services which you are qualified to perform
- Establishing reasonable and fair fees

- Promising only reasonable, achievable results
- Maintaining professional confidences and confidential material
- Meeting deadlines
- Maintaining open and timely communications with clients
- Admitting mistakes and working with the client to correct them

No personal or organizational code of ethics is foolproof, and certainly none fits every situation you'll encounter. But at the very least they provide a starting point for you to work out potential problem situations. And they may be a selling point you can offer clients that puts you a notch above your competition. It's another sign of your trust and integrity, and those are among the cornerstones of your new profession.

As I said at the start of this chapter, these are the finishing touches you need to consider before starting your new consulting business—the fine points that can help set you apart from millions of other consultants scrambling for clients.

GOOD LUCK TO MONICA DUBOIS AND AARON STEINBERG

Neither Monica nor Aaron had a problem with image. Both had an innate sense of professionalism and a well-developed professional persona. They looked like the experienced professionals they were.

Not only that, both chose to err—wisely—on the side of conservative restraint in their initial presentation materials, such as business cards and brochures.

Monica had a friend, a design student, who created several logo options. She finally decided that none of them exactly suited her and chose to wait on a logo. Instead, she expressed her creativity in her choice of colors: medium mauve with two eighth-inch-wide stripes underlining her business name. The stripes were khaki and deep, forest green. She felt the mauve expressed a capacity for feeling and emotion appropriate for an expert in human resources, while the khaki and forest green spoke of practicality and reliability. Besides, she decided, if none of that came across to prospective clients, at least it was quietly attractive and eye-catching, but not too wild and unorthodox.

Aaron opted for a version of the executive pin-stripe. He knew he didn't want a logo, because he didn't want to narrow himself into a confining image. So he chose off-white with black type and a quarter-inch gray stripe running vertically to the left of his business name. He felt it was conservative but expressive, elegant, and refined, but still interesting and arresting—everything he hoped his business would be.

Neither Monica nor Aaron saw the need to start out with a written code of ethics. Both felt they understood ethics, including business ethics, quite well, and didn't anticipate any problems. But about six months into consulting, Aaron had the occasion to reconsider.

A prospective client approached him, said Aaron had been recommended by a mutual friend, and asked Aaron meet with him to discuss a project. They met and spent several hours discussing the client's business needs. It was only at the end of that discussion that the client admitted he had already hired another consultant—whom Aaron knew well and occasionally worked with—to do the job. He said he was dissatisfied with the other consultant's work. He asked Aaron to consider stepping in and taking over.

It wasn't really a hard decision, but Aaron asked for a day to consider. Then he politely turned the client down. He advised the client to talk with his consultant openly about his concerns. Further, he said that if down the road the client and consultant could not work out their differences, and the client ended that relationship with a reasonable settlement for services already rendered, he would consider bidding on that project or a similar one.

He also suggested that in the future, the client advise a prospective consultant up front of such an ethical complication. It cost him money, but Aaron felt the price of the lost contract was worth the peace of mind he experienced in upholding his own ethical standards.

Monica and Aaron are now steaming along the road to great success and personal satisfaction. The road from here will not all be smooth. They'll hit their share of ruts and black ice, road blocks, and deadly detours. But they're on their way and enjoying every minute of it, and moreover, they're armed with most of the tools they'll need to deal with danger zones. As are you.

With what you've learned here and in the preceding chapters, your business should be a roaring success. Such a success, in fact, that your biggest worry in coming years may be whether or not you should expand. I'll discuss the pros and cons of growing your business in Chapter 10.

10

DECIDING WHETHER TO GROW

You're poised now for success. You can feel it, taste it. You want it, and want it badly. That's to be expected. No one starts a business hoping just to get by. All true entrepreneurs have a finely honed competitive spirit that helps them toil steadily toward success, through the inevitable ups and downs and the vicissitudes of the business world.

At some point, though, success can spell crisis for your business. That's because success and profitability usually mean growth, and you can only accept so much business before it becomes necessary to consider expanding your operations. After all, there's just so much one person can do in 24 hours. When you find you simply don't have enough time, you may have to turn away business, and that can mean watching your competitors latch firmly onto your prospective clients.

Success inevitably will bring you to the brink: to grow or not to grow. You may like your nice, tight operation, with only yourself to be concerned about. It's true that you don't have to grow. It's possible and permissible to remain small. But realize that if you remain a one-person operation, you may limit your earning power and your future.

There are a few ways around that: You can remain small but increase your earning power by increasing your fees. If you do that, however, you need to offer enhanced services for those higher fees, at least with your current clients. You'll need to create the perception, at least, that there's justification for the higher fees.

Another approach is to upgrade the quality of the clients you serve or the quality of the projects you undertake. If you're dealing with a medium-size company with good revenues rather than a small-size company with a small profit margin, you can charge more for what's essentially the same service.

Sooner or later, though, most successful entrepreneurs consider growing. But what's the best way to do it? Inevitably, growth necessitates more funds. And that can create a cash flow crisis. More important, how do you finance your expansion? Because, let's face it, any expansion costs money. The truth is, it takes more money to make more money. You may need to take on additional debt.

SOME THINGS TO CONSIDER ABOUT GROWTH

Before you decide whether to expand your consulting business, there are some things to consider. Once again you need to remember that as a freelance consultant you are the business. When clients retain The Ford Group, first and foremost they are retaining Lynda Ford. By some means or another they know or know of Lynda, and they know her skills and expertise. It's her they're hiring.

And, just as surely, when a client hires your business, that client will be hiring you and expecting service and face time from you, not from some anonymous employee. There are, of course, ways of dealing with that expectation, but it's a good idea to keep that expectation uppermost in your mind when you consider growing.

Then, consider the personal costs of expansion. One reason you started a home-based consulting business may have been for greater flexibility in your schedule, for more time to spend with your family. Are you ready to throw that flexibility and family time away, or at least restrict it even further? Because if you begin to expand, that's exactly what you'll be doing.

Sure, you'll be hiring both clerical and professional help, or making other professional partnership arrangements, but you'll be putting in more hours and overseeing more projects as well. There's no way around that. So be prepared for personal life changes, as well as professional ones.

Finally, real growth may mean you have to expand your home office or relocate. Chances are that if you hire another professional and office help, a move at some point will be inevitable. Most of us don't have the option of expanding our homes to accommodate a growing business. And even if our homes and families could adjust, chances are zoning restrictions would prohibit such expansion. So if you're thinking about serious growth, start checking into a good business location.

THERE ARE SEVERAL WAYS TO ENSURE GROWTH

Okay. After careful consideration you've decided it's time to expand. Clients are knocking on your door and you don't want to turn them away. To service them properly you're going to incur new expenses, so you want to be aggressive in seeking out new business in order to ensure that your additional income more than covers those increased expenses. You want to maintain your profit margin and even improve it. What do you do to ensure sufficient growth despite heavy competition? Consider the suggestions that follow.

Expand your list of services

One way to grow is to expand your service offerings. That way, you expand your niche and entice new clients to your door. You may have to take classes or additional training before you have the skills necessary to offer new services, but you may also be able to buy those services.

One way to do that is to hire, or take in, another professional who offers a different set of skills from those you possess. Make sure that the person's skills complement, rather than mirror, your own. And of course, investigate the person thoroughly to be sure he or she shares your work ethic and standards. This person will be representing you—and your business—so your reputation's on the line. But if you can find the right person, that's often the easiest way to expand your business's offerings.

Another way is to subcontract with another consultant for additional services as the need arises. Start by subcontracting small parts of a project to one or two consultants to try them out and make sure the fit works. Just as you would in hiring an employee, you need to be sure the subcontractors you work with are trustworthy, reliable, and share your work ethic and work standards. Remember that when you subcontract, you have to ensure quality control. That responsibility—the responsibility for the overall success of the project—is yours, and yours alone.

Or, you can establish a regular partnership agreement with several other consultants to provide a range of services useful to each of you. That way you don't lose your separate identities and client lists, but can offer a much wider range of services than otherwise possible.

Acquire another consulting business

While many types of businesses expand through acquisition, this option is used less frequently with consulting businesses because of the very personal, individual nature of the business.

However, it can be done. Remember Lynda Ford's consultant friend, who was ready to retire and handed her his client list? That was an acquisition of sorts, with the added benefit of coming at no cost to Ford.

You may not be lucky enough to be able to acquire a client list for free, but you may want to be on the lookout for an established consultant who is ready to chuck it or retire, and who has something—clients or staff or ongoing projects—worth something to you. Then, decide exactly how much it's worth to you and try to reach an agreement on that price.

Expand your market

Take what you do now and adapt it to other industries or markets. You'll have to be creative in many cases to make the leap, but remember: The problems, processes, and solutions for all businesses are much the same.

You'll have to learn the culture, lingo, and unique qualities and elements of each new industry you enter, but that can be done.

The key is to continue to do what it is you do best, but tailor it to suit a new industry.

Expand your coverage area

With the Internet, your target market, geographically speaking, can be the world. Historically, business started from the home area and then expanded outward geographically, staying within a reasonable traveling distance from the home base. Off-site, or satellite locations, could increase the coverage area, but that isn't really necessary for a consultant in today's electronic age.

Theoretically, at least, you can find and service your clients nationally and even internationally through electronic communications and through commercial business travel. If you're willing to hop on a plane or train, you can get almost anywhere in a time frame that can fit most business needs.

Consider going international

International consulting is no longer the special preserve of mega-consulting firms. More and more small and midsize firms—even one-person operations—are seeing the economic wisdom of expanding overseas. Communications technology and improved transportation systems have eased the way.

There are some risks involved, of course. Language barriers can be a problem, as can cultural differences. Law, politics, and environmental standards can be vastly different and daunting. Even the complexities of working in different time zones can cause unforeseen problems. You need to consider all of these factors—and figure out how to deal with them—before you enter the international fray.

Here are some specific things you should consider before you make a decision to go international:

1. How willing and able are you to travel?
2. How easily do you adapt to new and different environments?
3. How well/easily will your skills and services travel overseas?

In other words, is there a need for your services in other
countries?

4. Why should an international client hire you?

5. Do you have the time and energy to devote to international
   clients, with the travel, language, and cultural considerations
   that will complicate the relationship?

If you decide you'd like to forge ahead internationally, the next
step is to pick your markets. To do that, you should assess the
potential markets the same way you did when determining your
initial U.S. market. What's the competition? What's the demand
for your services? What's the cost for you to deliver those services
and how much can you charge for them? You want to figure out
which foreign markets offer you the most profit potential, with the
least government and legal interference.

And don't forget to assess the political situation in foreign markets carefully. Determine as best you can how stable the government is. You don't want to jump through all the legal and financial
hoops one government requires to do business there, only to find
that the government toppled and there's a whole new political
agenda to satisfy.

So where do you find all this information about foreign markets?
From a variety of governmental, trade, and professional associations, including the U.S. government, international organizations,
foreign governments, and trade associations.

The U.S. Government

The State Department can help you assess the political and economic conditions of countries you're interested in through its Bureau of Economic and Business Affairs and through U.S.
embassies around the world. The U.S. Government Printing Office
in Washington, D.C., publishes a biweekly newsletter called *Business America*, which is designed to help U.S. businesses compete
in foreign markets by providing them with up-to-date information.

The Department of Commerce also keeps track of the global
marketplace and can provide you with excellent information. Most
helpful will be the International Trade Administration, the Foreign

Commercial Service, and the Center for International Research. Specialists in these agencies can provide you with trade and economic data and can point you to appropriate sources of additional information not readily available.

The Small Business Administration also provides advice and aid to small businesses. It, too, has an Office of International Trade that can help you determine which markets are right for you and provide background and legal information on those markets. The U.S. Small Business Administration in Washington, D.C., also offers a publication, *Breaking Into the Trade Game*, which provides useful information.

International organizations

The United Nations publishes a number of reports and reference books that will provide you with excellent information on foreign markets, including the *International Trade Statistics Yearbook*, the *Demographic Yearbook*, and the *Statistical Yearbook*.

The World Bank was established to offer aid and economic development guidance and funds to Third World countries and is a wealth of information on economic and business activities in these and other countries around the world.

The Organization of Economic Cooperation and Development produces monthly statistical reports on foreign markets, foreign trade, productivity and employment levels, and wages and prices.

Foreign governments and trade associations

Contact foreign governments through their U.S. embassies and consulates for the quickest response time. They all have commercial attachés whose job it is to help foster foreign investment and business enterprise in their countries. They can help you through the governmental requirements and legal hazards and offer business tips, as well provide general market data.

Most trade and professional associations representing industries have a wealth of knowledge about foreign markets that you can access, either through their publications or directly from their association officials.

Many international commercial banks with U.S. and foreign branches can provide useful economic information.

U.S. Chambers of Commerce branches in foreign cities can also give you information on local economic and market conditions, as well as specific business leads and referrals.

FINANCING YOUR EXPANSION

Back when you were just starting your business I advised you to forget a business loan because banks don't lend to start-ups. They consider it too risky.

Well, times have changed. You're no longer a start-up and if you find it necessary to expand, you've mostly likely got a proven track record of success. This time, they'll consider you for a business loan. Chances are you won't need all that much money, since you still carry your inventory in your head, or perhaps now in yours and several others'. Maybe you'll need $5,000 to $10,000 for additional computer equipment. Or $15,000 to $50,000 to expand your home office into an office suite. Or to lease and outfit a new, commercial location.

Your best bets may still be a home equity or a personal loan. Again, base your choice on how much you need to borrow. If you need only a little, under $2,000, use credit cards; $2,000 to $10,000, take out a personal loan; if you need to borrow more, consider a home equity loan. But a commercial loan is an option, too.

You should search for a home equity loan and a personal loan exactly like you did for your first mortgage. Comparison shop for the best interest rates at banks, credit unions and savings and loans.

Your best bet for a commercial loan is a commercial bank, commercial lender or the Small Business Administration. Again, comparison shop for the best deal.

Commercial banks

Commercial banks usually offer cheaper interest rates than any of the other options. The main function of commercial bank financing is to provide short-term working capital for help with purchase of new equipment. Usually the loans are for a year or less, and the interest rate is generally just a bit above the prime interest rate.

Banks tend to prefer young and expanding—though not start-up—businesses that show steady and reliable revenues. They also prefer to lend to customers they know and with whom they do business, so first consider the bank at which you have your business and personal accounts. Your professional team can also be helpful with introductions and suggestions. Be aware that you may or may not have to put up collateral—something of corresponding value you pledge as security against repayment of the loan—on a commercial bank loan.

Each bank has its own unique procedures and lending policies, so make some calls to determine how receptive each bank might be to your particular loan application. Then check with your professional team and with your peers in the business community on the reputation of the bank and its loan officers.

Try to make a personal connection with the bank president or commercial loan officer. Ask for a brief get-acquainted meeting, or suggest you meet informally over coffee. You can learn a lot about how the bank and its personnel will treat your business and your loan by how they interact with you informally.

Commercial lenders

Many banks are affiliated with commercial lenders, so if you don't qualify for a bank loan, they may steer you to a commercial lender subsidiary. Your account or banker should also be able to recommend one.

Commercial lenders can be a good source of debt financing because they tend to be less conservative than commercial banks. While a commercial bank may not like the spotty look of a consultants' financial statement—with its feast or famine appearance—commercial lenders aren't quite so picky.

They're also willing to take greater risks, to offer longer term loans and often are open to some creative, flexible financing schemes. The trade-off is they charge higher interest rates and have bigger prepayment penalties than banks do. Plus, with commercial lenders collateral is always required.

Small Business Administration

The Small Business Administration has a number of different loan programs that can help with your expansion financing. Generally, you must have been rejected by at least three other financial institutions before you can apply for an SBA loan. There also are SBA loan guarantee programs that work with local banks to guarantee loans to small businesses. The drawbacks are that there's a long waiting list for SBA loans and daunting paperwork involved.

The interest rates for the SBA's direct loans are about at the market average, and may be made for terms of from five to fifteen years. Fixed-asset loans are also available from the SBA through its 503 Program, which provides long-term financing—for those rejected for other commercial financing—for equipment, building, and other fixed-asset purchases. The rates are below market rates, but the same problems with long waits and backbreaking paperwork demands apply.

The SBA guaranteed loans may be your best bet. Most SBA loans are made under this program, in which private lenders make loans that are guaranteed up to 80 percent by the SBA. There is no minimum-size loan amount, and the SBA provides special incentives to lenders who provide guaranteed loans of $50,000 or less, which is probably where your loan would fall.

HOW ONE EXPERT CONFRONTS THE GROWTH DILEMMA

Right now Chuck Monroe is struggling with the grow, no grow, or how-to-grow issue.

Monroe started his consulting business, Pegasus Organization, Inc., in Phoenix, Arizona, as a sole practitioner in 1991. That was after twenty-five rewarding years at IBM, RCA, and Digital Equipment Corp (DEC). He left the corporate world in the end because he didn't like what was happening there.

Now Monroe, who is active in the Institute of Management Consultants (IMC) and has taught the IMC three-day workshop, "Management Consultants, A Workshop for Professionals," does management consulting on strategic planning and business-to-business marketing and sales issues for commercial companies, predominantly high-tech and software companies. He also does some implementation of sales and marketing projects for clients.

Monroe said when he joined DEC in 1971, "It was a young company and fast-footed." But over the years that changed. With age, he said, the company's management became political and interested only in political solutions.

"DEC was to the point we had to rig sales forecasts to say what the upper management wanted to hear, so they became disconnected from reality. It was like the Southern California smog that got a little thicker each year so one ever noticed that eventually they never saw the sun again. I got tired of the stifling environment and took a buyout option in fall 1991."

That's when the sun started to shine again for Monroe. "Suddenly it was like I was reconnected with my intellect again and could be entrepreneurial. I was the only happy employee in the building from the time I gave notice until termination. I felt whole and creative again. Hallelujah! I was cured! I could see again!"

As a sole practitioner with a sub-S corporation, Monroe hires subcontractors as his business needs require, mostly clerical workers for list management and correspondence, telemarketers to do specific client campaigns, and researchers to do research and Internet legwork. At one time, he had subcontracted with as many as twenty-two contractors. More typical, he said, is one to two. He has also partnered some projects with other consultants on a peer basis.

The good news is his business has grown "with each year surpassing the prior and gross exceeding any pay I ever received from a corporation."

The bad news? "It has reached a plateau where I would like to clone myself to keep growing revenue. I have an aversion to putting someone on the payroll as an employee permanently. Most consultants reach this plateau—there are only so many hours in the day—and realize they need a product to leverage their income so they come up with books, tapes, seminars to sell.

"This is the point where quality-of-life issues come up. How much is my intellectual freedom to do my best work worth, versus a more 'normal' life?" Monroe and his wife adopted an infant in spring 1997, and he's no longer willing or able to pull all-nighters to get assignments out on time.

Monroe said he doesn't yet have an answer to the growth versus quality-of-life issue because the results aren't in on some experiments he is doing as alternative strategies to "ramp up" his consulting practice.

He noted, too, that ramping up may be interpreted different ways, such as: increasing gross revenues; increasing net revenues (which is very different from increasing gross revenues—"It's not how much you make, it's how much you keep."); increasing the quality of clients or assignments; increasing the effectiveness of the service delivery; creating additional products to sell along with the service delivery ("Products have an economic leverage that services do not.").

"If one increases revenues through more billing hours by using additional people to do service delivery, quality of service delivered *and* quality of life may go down," Monroe said. "One way to increase billings without increasing billing hours is to upscale clients or services."

Another approach is to move into speaking as a source of revenue and to generate clients for upscale consulting engagements. But, as Monroe points out, "The travel involved in this strategy obviously has an impact on quality of life."

Monroe said he's working in several of these areas and is waiting to see which path produces the best results for him personally.

"For example, I have six articles coming out in the first quarter of 1998 designed to increase my desirability as a speaker. I am also engaging in some specific publicity/promotional work that I haven't done before. A fellow consultant who has developed a 'talking model' for strategic planning and execution is asking me to partner with him and start a firm (with a possible high impact on personal freedom). And I am looking at shifting my practice and client profile slightly to moderately.

"The bottom line is I need to evolve my practice or professional focus and I am now in a transitional period to see what works."

Before getting to this grow, no grow, or how-to-grow brink, Monroe went through the usual consultant's trials: feast and famine of assignments; taking assignments he didn't want just to fill the lulls; spreading himself too thin on nonfocus engagements before getting the business to the point where he could focus on the assignments he preferred.

To those of you just beginning on this journey and not yet worrying about growth, he had the following advice. Some of it will by now sound familiar, but it's worth repeating here:

Have a marketing and business plan before starting the business.

Review the plan with an experienced consultant before starting out.

Start sales and marketing before quitting your day job

"It's surprising," he said, "how many consultants don't have a plan. Most of the people sincerely entering the profession as sole practitioners know their discipline cold and are qualified to deliver their service, but they are clueless on sales and marketing. They know they have the world's best new hammer and don't know why everyone doesn't hire them to bang on nails."

11

THE SECRETS TO SUCCESS

Congratulations. By now you're well on your way to entrepreneurial success. This chapter provides a summary of the key things a new entrepreneur needs to keep in mind as she develops her business. It offers you reminders—sound advice you can refer to at any time, no matter how far along you are.

SETTING UP SHOP

Determine whether you have what it takes

Making the decision to be a freelance consultant is a big step. Your whole future is at stake. Some people have what it takes to be an entrepreneur, but frankly, some don't. So the first thing you need to do is determine whether you really have what it takes to become a successful entrepreneur.

To do that you need to find out more about yourself, your likes and dislikes, work preferences, and character traits. You may think you already know all that, but after taking the attitudinal self-checkup and the Entrepreneurial Aptitude Test in Chapter 1, you may be surprised. So before you take any irrevocable steps toward starting your own consulting business, take these self-analysis tests. Your answers to those questions can help you avoid financial disaster. And if you decide to go ahead, they'll help you build the foundation for your future consulting success.

Focus your business: find a niche

Far too many consultants have a general set of skills and a vague notion of what they can do for clients but never really find a unique focus for their business that they can market effectively. Or even explain effectively.

You need to figure out exactly what it is you want to do for clients, and what you are able to do for them. Decide what services or products you will provide, then figure out how to explain your business in two sentences or less.

To help in this task, define your ideal client. Who out there would be interested in buying such a service or product? Where do you find those prospective clients? What is the potential size of that target market? If you have trouble coming up with good answers, narrow your focus. Zero in on an industry or business and figure out exactly how you can help that business grow or increase sales. What can you do for the client that he can't do for himself or that you can do better or cheaper or more efficiently?

Remember, many consultants continue to refine or alter their business focus for several years, as they become more experienced in consulting, and as the needs of the marketplace change. And that's good. You need to be flexible and adaptable to survive in the business world—you've already figured that out if you're reading this book.

But even at the outset, to make the biggest bang in the marketplace you can, you're going to need a good, tight focus and as unique a niche as you can find.

Consider basing your business at home

You can save a lot of money by basing your consulting business at home, but first you need to be sure it's the right fit for your personality, your family and your business and client needs.

Many people revel in the freedom and flexibility working at home brings. They want to be able to work flexible hours and as long or little as they choose. They also like the idea of being physically closer to their families.

But for many, that freedom can spell disaster. Without a boss setting their schedule and turning off the office lights, many workaholics simply aren't able to turn off the computer, shut their home office door, and return to their personal lives. Others can't escape the many distractions around home that threaten their concentration and business success.

Before you make any decision on a home business, check out the pros and cons and the list of what you'll need in your home office in Chapter 5.

Create a business plan and marketing plan

Again, do your homework before you leap. Whether you've been downsized out of work and are feeling panicky—especially if you're feeling panicky—or just ready to make a career change, you need to act in a careful, rational, thoughtful manner as you start on this venture. Untoward haste now will cost you in bucks and peace of mind later.

First you need to do some quick math to determine how much you can reasonably earn at the start; compare that to what you need to live on. If there's a gap, figure out how you can cover it. You'll find information on how to do this and the rest of the homework you need to accomplish in Chapter 3.

A business plan and a marketing plan are a must. Far too many new consultants ignore these basics and end up paying the price. When you prepare your plans, get help, either before you start or after you've put them together. Run them by another consultant you trust, your attorney, your accountant, and other small business owners. Also get help and a critique from SCORE volunteers.

Use all the resources available to you, especially those that are free. And then, listen carefully, thoughtfully, to what these experts have to say. Don't make this a pro forma exercise, something you've read you should do but don't take seriously. And don't put those plans on a dusty shelf once they're finished. You should refer to your business and marketing plans regularly as you establish and operate your business.

Leap into the information age

Telecommunications has set new standards for small business. Your clients and contacts not only expect you to have a telephone, but a fax machine and some form of messaging service as well. The fax is a necessary convenience for the timely sharing of documents and correspondence. You'll need an answering machine or voice mail service to avoid missing calls and sales. These are the minimum requirements for today's small business.

But you should go even further. Jump into the information age, if you haven't already. The computer has become a necessary tool for small business success, not just a luxury or an expensive toy. In order to gain the full benefit of computer technology you must know what to choose and how to use it efficiently. And that involves much more than turning on a computer and typing a letter.

The right hardware and software can mean doing in minutes what used to take hours, or even days. It also can be an easy, efficient, direct lifeline to your client. First, however, you'll need to identify the specific technology that will help your business. When evaluating the range of options, weigh the merits of each against these considerations:

1. Will the tool or service enable you to make more productive use of your time?
2. Will it enable you to do a better job of what you're already doing?
3. Can you use it to broaden your reach in the marketplace?
4. Does it improve client service by reducing response time or giving clients better access to you?
5. Will the technology pay for itself in cost savings, increased productivity, or expanded sales opportunities?

It's important to tailor the technology mix to your business operation. List every task your business performs during a given day and consider whether technology can help you accomplish that task more efficiently or productively. Only invest in the tools for which you have a proven use. Then expand your capabilities as your needs evolve.

If you're not sure whether a specific technology will help you, do some experimenting. Most reputable computer and office equipment companies will offer free demonstrations and trials.

Why invest in something when you're not sure it offers the

solutions you need? For telecommunications services such as an 800 toll-free number, conference calling, and E-mail, it's easy and inexpensive to experiment with your options. Sign up for these services and track the results for a couple of months. If they're effective, keep the service; if not, cancel it.

With hardware, the up-front investment is more substantial. And there's always the likelihood this year's breakthrough will be quickly outdated. If you're watching your budget, leasing equipment may make more sense than outright purchase, at first. Try now, buy later: It's an inexpensive way to sample technology before its benefits are proven.

But if you decide to buy, do it right. Mapping out your expectations will simplify your job. Then just match software and hardware to your needs, watch out for a few common pitfalls, and you'll be fine.

GETTING BUSINESS

"Sell yourself" to ensure success

As an entrepreneur, every time you sell your service you're selling yourself. To ensure success, you need to be sure that your selling technique is personal—an intimate, personal exchange of ideas and services between you and the client. The only way to keep clients is to provide expertise and quality service. But you'll be even more successful if they feel that your warmth and character and your honesty and integrity are part of the bargain.

Building trust takes time. But when you're trying to persuade a client you're the right consultant for the job—in other words, trying to make a sale—time is short. Therefore it's important to know shortcuts. People instinctively trust someone they believe cares for them. In demonstrating you care you'll foster that feeling of trust. Here are some keys to creating a caring environment:

Appearances count. You should dress appropriately for your type of consulting business, when you're not at your home office or when it's likely you'll encounter clients. Regardless of what you wear, it should be neat, clean, and simple, not fussy. Pay careful attention to your grooming. Be businesslike. Keep your office clean and comfortable.

Make your greeting count. Getting off to the right start is crucial. Greet clients warmly. Smile, shake hands, and be sure to look them in the eye. Greet them by name if you can. Introduce yourself by name if you can't.

Don't rush to business. Engage the client in pleasant conversation by asking questions. Try to find common ground, even if it's the weather. It's the thought that counts, not the scintillating conversation.

Be responsive. Don't try to do two things at once when you're greeting the client. You can't answer the phone or solve another client's problem mentally while a client is trying to carry on a conversation. Lean forward when she's talking and acknowledge what she's saying by nodding your head. Be expressive. Be animated.

Telephones aren't anonymous. Treat telephone communications as you would face-to-face meetings: Be warm and cordial, be personal, engage in brief pleasantries.

Be courteous. It may save time, but will cost you business if you forget the little courtesies in the crush of business. Don't forget to say please and thank you.

In the end, your goal is not just to clinch a contract, but to keep a client by building client loyalty. So an important part of your job will be not only your relationship with the client during the course of the assignment, but your follow-up after the project is completed. That means you need to ask the client for feedback, both positive and negative.

You should also keep in touch after the project by communicating regularly with clients. Let them know what exciting things you're doing (without giving away secrets, of course) and what new services you're offering. Drop them a line (your new computer equipment will help) to check on their progress with your service. Your goal is to make each client feel special. Make them feel you truly have their interests at heart. And you should—because their interests are your interests. Their continued loyalty will help your business to grow.

Dealing with complaints.   Every consultant makes mistakes. Every entrepreneur has at least one dissatisfied client. Sometimes the fault is genuinely yours or your employee's. Other times the client is wrong.

Your job, regardless of who's at fault, is to turn a no-win situation into a win-win one by responding promptly to client complaints. Remember, the only way for you to win is to ensure that the client is never wrong. So you need to demonstrate how deeply you care about what has gone wrong and how committed you are to making things right. Do whatever it takes to resolve the situation to the client's satisfaction. Then, follow up to make sure the client remains satisfied. Make sure she's aware that you really are concerned and want her to remain a good client. Personal selling comes down to common sense. It's nothing new and it's no gimmick. But it's amazing how many otherwise savvy consultants forget the basics in the heat of the daily business grind. Don't let that happen to you.

Become a skilled interviewer

All consultants, like other business owners, need good interviewing skills, both for interviewing clients to get at the substance of their needs and in the event you decide to expand and hire.

However, few of us have obtained the skills needed to become effective interviewers. Managers are not ordinarily taught these skills. While it's not terribly difficult to determine a job candidate's technical expertise, that's not usually why one fails at a new job. New hires generally fail because they can't work as part of a team, they're not flexible, or because their expectations about recognition, environment, or management style haven't been met.

The same goes for prospective clients. You need to be able to read between the lines when you interview them—or when you interview each other—to get at what their real needs are and whether they really can work well with an outsider.

Good interview skills can heighten your awareness of areas of strengths or weaknesses or simply sound the alarm that this is not a good fit. One word of caution, however: While you'll be asking a lot of questions, keep your mouth shut as much as possible. You'll learn more and evaluate better by simply listening.

The following questions are designed to help you make some decisions about a job candidate's appropriateness. Many of these questions, some with a bit of massaging, can also offer you insight into a prospective client's style.

1. Describe an instance where you used an unusual solution to solve a common problem. This will give you some insight into the candidate's creativity and willingness to take risks relative to problem-solving ability.

2. What do you believe is the personal profile for someone to be successful at this job? The answer gives you some idea of how close the candidate's ideas are to your views on what's required to be successful. It also gives you insight into what the candidate believes are the key responsibilities of the job.

3. Describe a situation in which you were a member of a team but disagreed with the way others wanted to approach a project. This helps to give you some idea of the candidate's teamwork skills and ability to communicate ideas and how he approaches conflict and resolution.

4. Define cooperation. This will give you more information on the candidate's ability to work as part of a team.

5. Give an example of a time you needed to understand the position of another in order to get your work done. How did you go about getting that understanding? The answer will show whether the candidate considers the opinions of others and the effect that his decisions have on others. Is the candidate's style autocratic or participatory?

6. What do you consider a positive work environment? This answer shows whether the candidate will be comfortable in your environment. If the answer describes an environment unlike yours, forget it.

7. Describe the best and worst boss you ever had. This example can give you information about the candidate's expectations on how he should be managed and usually gives you an idea of how the candidate will manage others.

8. How would your subordinate describe your strengths and weaknesses? This question addresses the candidate's self-awareness, confidence, honesty, and sensitivity to others.

9. What do you think are the traits of the ideal manager? This question will provide you with information on the candidate's philosophy and expectations.

10. Describe a mistake you made in your last position and what you learned from it. This discussion will give you some insight into the candidate's self-awareness, analytical ability, problem-solving ability, and objectivity.

11. Describe a situation in which you had to make a difficult decision. This exchange will demonstrate the candidate's willingness to do the right thing even when it might result in an unpopular outcome. This, in turn, will also demonstrate the candidate's strength of convictions.

12. What are you most passionate about? This question will address the candidate's motivation, intensity, and priorities.

13. How would you define success in life? This question will give you a view of the candidate's personal and professional priorities, values, sense of life balance, motivation, and maturity.

14. When you're not working, how do you spend your time? The activities the candidate describes reflect personal style and mutual areas of comfort.

15. What books have you read? How have they affected you?

These answers will give you some idea of what intellectually stimulates and challenges the candidate.

16. What personal characteristics sometimes interfere with the way you work? This question will give you insight into the candidate's self-awareness and honesty.

17. Could you describe your ideal job? This inquiry will demonstrate the candidate's creativity, insight into personal and professional needs, expectations, and motivation.

18. How do you plan your day? This question will indicate how the candidate handles time management, "prioritization," and flexibility.

Turn yourself into an expert

You'll need to "credentialize" yourself as an expert in your field. Your previous experience as an employee will be helpful in this, particularly if you can point to specific projects you led or get testimonials from previous clients or coworkers.

You also can establish yourself as an expert by writing articles and books, making speeches at seminars, conventions, and local business groups, teaching classes, and giving interviews to the media. Make sure you're seen and heard whenever and wherever your area of expertise is being discussed.

Then network. Join the Kiwanis and Rotary and attend informal Business After Hours get-togethers. Hand out your business card. But also touch base regularly with former professors and classmates, former coworkers, and clients. You need to create an image of yourself as a respected leader in the field, so that when there's a need for someone who does what you do, your name will be at the top of the list.

Polish your business image

Here are some ways to make sure your business image is positive.

Pay attention to your telephone answering system. The telephone is the most powerful tool a small business has. It's a lifeline to clients, vendors, and other professionals. And while it may be physically impossible for you to be available at the other end of the line twenty-four hours a day, you want those trying to reach you to feel like you are.

That's why the telephone answering system you choose is vital. It must convey to clients that you're interested in their needs and desires. That way they'll be more likely to leave a message. "Hang-ups" are more than a nuisance, they represent lost business. Here are some suggestions:

1. Ideally, your telephone should be answered by a knowledgeable member of your support staff. There's nothing like a caring, competent person servicing the lines to instill confidence in clients.

2. Answering services are generally the worst option. The operator often knows nothing about the business, and it shows. It's easier and faster to leave a message on a machine than with an individual who may stumble over terminology and names.

3. The advances in communications technology make voice mail systems a good compromise for small companies that cannot afford support staff. However, these systems must be caller friendly and simple to maneuver through.

4. The outgoing message should be in your voice. Your tone and inflection must encourage those who would otherwise hang up to leave a message.

5. Consider recording a new message daily that contains the day and date. This indicates you use the system regularly.

6. Be informative but brief. Let callers know you're on another line or out, but that you regularly retrieve messages and will respond as soon as possible.

Business cards leave a visual imprint. Your stationery and business cards are not only vital tools for conveying information about your business to clients, they're also tools for demonstrating the high level of your professionalism. Here are some suggestions for making the most of them.

• Logos and designs can add unnecessary cost to the production of cards and stationary because, to be effective, they need to be professionally designed. Logos can also be too "busy" to read quickly, and riskier in terms of the type of impression they're likely to make. If they don't appeal to your clients' tastes, they may be a turnoff. Finally, it takes much time and money for a logo to become a real identifier for a business. For a small company this may not be practical.

• Instead, keep things simple. A clean layout and crisp type are not only easy to read but show you to be a sophisticated and savvy businessperson.

• Use a typeface, or font, that reflects your business. For example, stark, block letters for a technologies consultant, or a simple script for a tax consultant.

• In general, engraved stationery and cards are not worth the expense. Use quality paper that has some texture to it. A water mark is nice but not essential.

• Desktop publishing cards and stationery are efficient but effective only if the print quality is high. Amateur printing will negatively affect your business.

• If you farm out the printing don't buy too much at once. You may save money buying in bulk, but a new business usually changes cards and stationery within the first few years.

Focus on public relations

As advertising costs have continued to rise over the years, companies have turned more and more to no-cost public relations. That's because it has a proven track record for getting your message to target audiences, increasing sales, encouraging purchase and consumer satisfaction, creating and sustaining company image, and enhancing trust in you and your business.

However, not every business is ready to enter into the competitive world of public relations. There's nothing more dangerous for a company than presenting itself or a new product to the scrutiny of the public and the media before everything is absolutely ready to go.

Here are a few questions to consider before embarking on a public relations program:

1. Does your company have a mission statement?

2. What is the service, product, or announcement that defines your publicity campaign?

3. Have you outlined your target audience and do you know the target media that services those consumers?

4. Do you have a product image or spokesperson to represent the company and deliver its message?

5. Can you pinpoint easily what makes your company stand out against its competitors?

6. What, if any, are the misconceptions of your company in the marketplace and can you rebut them?

7. What is the weak point of your company and can you respond to it?

8. Do you have the right resources and the appropriate number of people to handle the requests that will result from the publicity?

9. Is this the best time to embark on a public relations campaign?

If you can successfully answer all of the questions above, your company should be ready to consider a public relations program. Remember, publicity works best when it's integral to the company's marketing, sales strategy, and image.

Create a mission statement. All effective publicity begins with a clear understanding of the company's mission. Often overlooked, it is the most concise way a company can define its relationship with its various publics and reveals much about the company's culture and marketing orientation.

Create press materials. Develop written materials that include: services, product, or company announcements; ''backgrounder'' on the company and its principals (with bios); a question-and-answer sheet with the designated expert; topics of discussion for interviewers; praise sheets and/or sell sheets; positive print coverage on the company and/or product; bio of spokesperson; and targeted pitch letters for the media. These press kits can be accompanied with video footage to highlight the announcement.

Contact targeted television, radio, and print media. Research media and develop a database; create your targeted pitch and backup strategy; and, most important, follow up. Make yourself available to tour your target markets for greater visibility. Consider radio giveaways.

Create an event. This helps market your company, product, or service directly to the public and provides an angle for press coverage. Tie the function to current events or news stories, holidays, or anniversaries. Involve local or national celebrities, or feature a contest to involve your constituency.

Write a bylined article or op-ed piece. If you can't get the media to write about your company then take matters into your own hands. Provide your trade or targeted consumer magazine with an article that will position you as an expert in the field. The op-ed piece should present a formal point of view or debate that can platform your company's message.

Speak to local business groups, consumer groups, and clubs. Talk to any group that will have you. More groups than you would imagine are on the lookout for a new face to speak on a wide variety of issues related to their lives, not just to their specific field of interest.

Develop a client newsletter and business brochure or manual. These will help you communicate regularly with committed and potential clients about news, products, and services of interest to them. Create a short response questionnaire for potential clients to comment on needs and preferences, then add their names to your mailing list.

Gain endorsements and awards for your company. Focus attention on your company by getting a high-profile association, publication, or person to give a stamp of approval.

While there's no magic involved, there is an art to getting your message out effectively. Here are seven general tips to help you communicate better with clients and target clients:

1. Make your position clear. What sets your company apart in the eye of the beholder? Do you really offer better services or products? More "bang per buck" in value provided? Do you have a "service edge"? Whatever it is, articulate it and communicate it, through as many avenues as you can, in brochures, sales presentations, articles, and advertising, so your clients start to remember it.

2. Become known as an expert. A little positive publicity goes a long way, especially if it's seen by prospective clients. Daily newspapers and industry trade reporters are always on the lookout for new sources for stories and comments. Get to know a few of them. Be accessible. Often, those quoted are the ones who respond the fastest to the reporters, rather than the most expert.

3. Don't shoot from the hip. Getting an opportunity to be quoted in the media is great—but you can blow it if you aren't schooled in being quotable. At minimum make sure you rehearse communicating key messages about the company. Consider working with a media consultant to construct all messages—written or oral— and to enhance your interview skills.

4. Increase strength through numbers. Small businesses often find it too expensive to buy advertising, create big events, sponsor seminars, and undertake other publicity activities. Try getting a group of small businesses together, either through the Chamber of Commerce, or other local business groups or informally on your own. Form your own network to make group purchases and hold mutually beneficial group events.

5. A picture is worth more than a thousand words. With our shorter and shorter attention spans, people will look at a great photograph before reading a lot of words. You can expand the impact of media coverage of a particular event, product, or service through interesting photography. It's worth the investment to use top professional photographers.

6. Mail to your friends. Create your own mailing list of business contacts—prospects, suppliers, clients, investors, etc.—and send information to them regularly. For example, inexpensive reprints of articles about your company or services, new brochures, and even letters providing an update on your business's progress are appropriate. Include a return post card, which enhances follow-up. Mail with regularity—quarterly or even monthly. Don't stop if the initial return is not high. Images are built and many sales made through cumulative impact.

7. A note of thanks. You can create good word-of-mouth publicity through strong "customer service" policies—from thank-you letters to clients to rapid response to client inquiries and complaints. Train personnel to be gracious no matter how trying the situation. This is a must and will go a long way toward fostering those warm and fuzzy feelings that keep clients coming back. It's not the quantity of activities, but the quality that counts. Select a small number of activities and commit the time to get them done, rather than biting off more than you can chew. It's important to stick with the effort, year after year, for it to have an impact on your business's image.

Here are ten more specific tips for getting publicity.

1. Support local charities by donating your services.
2. Support local charities by donating your time.
3. Obtain endorsements from clients.
4. Participate in local business initiatives and organizations.
5. Create a businessperson's association.
6. Work with civic organizations.
7. Become active in local politics and the school board.

8. Befriend the local media.

9. Contribute to, and endorse, local political candidates.

10. Network with, and support, community religious organizations.

Learn how to market yourself

Marketing isn't something you stick in your plan and on your calendar to do once a month, like paying the bills. Marketing should permeate your life. Just about everything you do should, in one way or another, become a marketing opportunity.

Remember: As a business consultant, you're your greatest business asset, and one you should present to the business community and to your general community as often as possible. You should maximize every encounter. Every chance you have to meet someone or greet someone—whether a businessperson or someone related to a businessperson or just another community resident—is a marketing opportunity, so make the most of it.

That doesn't mean forcing a business conversation or foisting your business materials on someone at an inopportune time. It means taking the trouble to introduce yourself and, if appropriate, your business name in a charming and gracious manner. You want to give people a reason to remember your name, face, and smile, and the memory should elicit the feeling that they had a pleasurable personal encounter with you. From there it's a short step to recalling your name in a business context should they need your services down the road.

There are also certain inexpensive marketing tricks you can use. Writing books and articles, teaching courses, and making presentations not only helps establish you as an expert in your field— they're also marketing opportunities, so use them as such. Join and attend professional associations, workshops, and seminars— that's marketing, too.

Become active in the community by attending community events, Chamber of Commerce meetings, Business After Hours social groups. Join Rotary, the Parent Teacher Association at your child's school, the board of directors of the local symphony. Make sure you're seen at, and become actively involved in, groups and events at which people gather.

The more prospective clients see you as a well-rounded, active, involved human being, the more likely they'll be to turn to you when their business needs a consultant's help.

MONEY ISSUES

Take steps to ensure payment

Consultants, like other small business owners, often find their most difficult, most onerous task is getting paid for their work. And that of course causes cash flow problems. There are some steps you should take to help ensure you're paid in a timely manner.

First, it's essential to get as much information as possible on clients before contracting to work for them. Talk to others with whom the client regularly interacts, either vendors, suppliers, customers, or clients. Find out what kind of person the client is and whether he pays his bills.

If necessary, run a credit check on any prospective client before signing a contract. Contact one of the following credit rating agencies and order a copy of the client's credit report: Trans Union, 800-916-8800; TRW, 800-682-7654; or Equifax, 800-685-1111.

Knowing your client is the best insurance you can have that you'll be paid in a timely way. But there are other things you can do as well. It's important to get a vendor number at the outset of the project. Many corporate accounts-payable departments require that you have a vendor number before they will issue you a check. Even if they don't require it, many such departments are a morass of bureaucracy and confusion and that number can speed the payment process immeasurably.

Get an advance. This is sometimes harder to do when you're first starting out, but it's not something you can afford to be squeamish about. You know how much your time is worth and how well you do your job. Be confident and be firm. As one professional businessperson to another, a reasonable client will understand your requirement for an advance.

Make it a standard part of your contract that you be paid at least 10 percent of your fee in advance. You may want to require more than 10 percent, but 10 percent is a minimum.

Use your contract.   Use your contract as another tool to help ensure you're paid. Make sure the contract states your fee arrangement and the timing of your payment schedule. The contract should also spell out your penalty for late payment. That should be at least 1½ percent a month for payments thirty-one days overdue. That way the client knows you mean business.

The contract should list the kinds of expenses the client will pay and any limits on those expenses. It should also specify that the client arranges and pays directly for all of your travel expenses. That will avoid the possibility of after-the-fact wrangles over travel fares.

Begin collection efforts the day after payments are due.   This shows you're in earnest about getting paid on time, and it will most likely result in your getting paid ahead of the rest of the pack. Don't wait until the account becomes seriously delinquent. Not only can this destroy cash flow, but it increases the odds of nonpayment.

Start your collection efforts with a friendly reminder.   There's no need to be hostile or threatening in the beginning. If the first reminder you send fails to yield payment, send another copy of the invoice, along with a cover letter stating that you thought it important to put in writing your understanding of the situation to date. The subtext, of course, is that you're creating a paper trail should you need to bring the person to court.

Close with a heartfelt hope that the situation is remedied as soon as possible. Most clients will respond to the implied threat.

You may need to use a collection service.   As a professional, you don't want to be in the business of hounding people for overdue bills. Bill-collecting takes time, energy, and persistence, not to mention persuasive skills. And it doesn't do anything for your professional image. It's a job, frankly, best left to lawyers and collection agents, even though they charge hefty fees ranging from 20 to 50 percent of funds collected.

Once an account is more than thirty days past due you should begin considering handing it over to someone else for collection. Some businesses routinely put all bills forty-five days past due in for collection, while others wait until ninety days have past.

Settle or get out.   As an alternative to a collection agent, you may want to consider settling with a delinquent client for a lesser amount, or agreeing to an extended payment schedule.

If a client still delays or refuses payment despite the above precautions, quit in the middle of the project or refuse further work from the client.

Collect accounts receivable faster

As a small business entrepreneur, it's always in your best interest to have as much cash available as possible. One way of maximizing your working capital is expediting the accounts-receivable process. For example: standard business practice requests client payments after thirty days. But if you were to alter the payment terms to fifteen days—or less—it could substantially lessen your need to borrow money and increase cash flow. That money could be used in any way you see fit: to pay bills or even to expand your business. Below are some other ways to help put the cash in your hands, where it belongs.

Invoice immediately.   Too often, businesses wait to send out their bills, virtually guaranteeing a slowdown in the payment cycle. Send out your invoice as soon as possible. While clients may be reluctant to pay right away, you've at least gotten the billing cycle under way.

Try to negotiate longer terms on your accounts payable.   Trying to slow down payment of accounts payable should be a part of your accounts receivable collection efforts. Find out if your vendors will accept payment within sixty days rather than the standard thirty. Suppliers in highly competitive industries are most likely to agree to this.

Set your fees right

Fee setting is where many new consultants—in fact most new business owners—are most insecure, and therefore where they make some of their worst mistakes. In short, most entrepreneurs set their prices too low. Worried about making sales, some entrepreneurs set their prices according to what their competitors are charging, some try just to make a "reasonable" profit for their time after costs, and some cut fees nearly to the bone in the hope of attracting more clients.

None of these are methods you should emulate. Setting fees too low may cause clients to assume your services are inferior to the competition. In addition, you may not be able to survive long enough to compete with more established consultants who can set fees lower because of greater volume.

How, then, should you determine the right price for your services?

1. Figure out your costs.

2. Figure out how much income you need.

3. Choose a pricing strategy.

4. Convince yourself to act with confidence, patience, and pride— and aim high because when you set a price, you also set an image for your business.

Determining costs. To figure out your costs, you need to tally three factors: material and supplies costs; labor costs, which should include your income plus benefits as well as those of any employees; and overhead costs, or the indirect costs of everything else, such as clerical and janitorial expenses, taxes, depreciation, and so on.

Pricing strategies. You have three pricing strategies to choose from. Comparable pricing—setting fees close to your competitor's fees works only when both firms are established. When you are the new business on the block, comparable pricing will not give your competitor's clients any reason to switch to you. Low pricing—as discussed above, in most cases, this method is a fatal mistake. High pricing—the best option for a new small business, high pricing reflects an image of quality, distinguishes you from your competitor, and helps you recover start-up costs quickly.

EXPANDING

Hire temps whenever possible

Temporary employees are a solution for many growing businesses not ready to make long-term employment commitments. If an agency is used, there are no costly benefits to absorb, no payroll taxes to pay, and no tax forms to be filed.

Finding the right temp is challenging and often daunting. There are essentially two ways: Do it yourself or hire an agency. No matter which way you choose to go, the one thing to remember is that the better you craft the job description of the position you are seeking to fill, the more likely it is you'll find a successful temp.

Doing it yourself can be problematic, but if it's the way you want to go, here are some essential tips to live by when finding a temp:

1. Search your own network. Often the best source for candidates is not a newspaper campaign, but personal referrals from current employees, friends, and other business peers. An excellent source of candidates can also be local college bulletin boards.

2. Weed out candidates. Two immediate ways to help sift through the résumés and begin the screening process are to set aside any résumés that have unexplained chronological gaps, typographical errors, or grammatical mistakes. While cover letters may not be an essential requirement for the job you're filling, they can often be a good indicator of the individual's accuracy and meticulousness.

3. Make your own appointments. Don't delegate the task—no matter how tedious—of scheduling the interview appointments for the candidates that interest you. It can be enlightening to speak directly with the candidate: The impression you receive on the telephone is the impression your clients will be receiving.

4. Focus on the candidate's past and your needs. The important questions to ask in the interview should focus on the candidate's past job performance and present needs. Three essential questions: Why do you choose to temp? Why did you leave your last permanent position? Why does this temp position appeal to you?

5. Always ask for references, and check them. This means actually speaking directly with previous employers and asking them pointedly whether this person is qualified. Find out about the candidate's past performance and attitude on the job. It's important for you to ask the previous employer if she would rehire the candidate.

Although using an agency can be more costly, it can save you time in the long run. You'll be putting yourself in the hands of professionals who make it their business to screen candidates and find the right individual for the job you're seeking to fill.

1. Shop agencies. Agencies should undergo the same scrutiny as a potential employee. Ascertain how long they've been in business. Be certain the agency screens and tests skills and scrutinizes references. Try to get a guarantee. There are a range of fees—check them in advance and compare them with other agencies.

2. Establish a strong rapport with the agency recruiter. A good one-on-one relationship will help the agency fulfill your needs. Have the recruiter visit your business premises and introduce him to other employees. Let the recruiter get a good sense of what a workday is like.

3. Be explicit about your expectations for the job and the company policies. Accurate job descriptions are critical, as is a complete list of the technical skills required such as computer software, typing, dictation, etc. Be clear about dress code, smoking policies, and other office regulations.

4. Realize that you get what you pay for. Temps are paid according to their skills. If you ask for a lesser rate, you should reduce your expectations for production.

5. When temps arrive be sure to acclimate them. Tell them what you want done for the day, where to find things (coffee, rest room, supplies), and when to break for lunch. If treated like semipermanent employees, they will perform best.

Think before you grow

Think long and hard before you make the decision to expand your business. As a consultant, clients are hiring you and your expertise and experience. Many of them won't have the same feelings of trust and confidence in an employee or junior partner.

But as your business grows—if you're as good as you think you are and follow this book, step-by-step—you'll find at some point that you have more business than you can handle. And you'll have to decide whether to grow, and if so, how to do it painlessly.

Subcontract parts of projects. Find someone whose work you're somewhat familiar with and subcontract pieces of projects to him or her, one by one, so you can check the work and act in a quality control capacity. In that way, too, you can get a feel for how the person works and whether you might make a good team permanently—either as a regular subcontractor or as a partner.

Hire someone who adds skills. If you decide to hire a subcontractor or take on a partner, be sure you choose someone who adds to your skill set rather than duplicating your own. If you find someone who complements what you know and do best, but brings additional knowledge and skills to your company, you can expand the list of products and services you offer clients and attract even more business.

THE FINISHING TOUCHES

Build a solid relationship with your client

When you are the business, the relationship you share with your client is the key to success. That relationship must be one of mutual trust and respect. Obviously, if a client hires you, you have already earned a measure of his respect and trust. But to complete the project successfully, it's important the client trusts and respects your professional decisions as well. That means he can't be constantly second-guessing you and questioning your judgment.

By the same token, if you have little trust in and respect for the client, you're going to have trouble completing the assignment successfully. In order to avoid troublesome relationships with the client, know who you're dealing with from the start. Investigate the prospective client and get to know him as well as possible under the circumstances.

Then be sure the project involves a problem you can solve—that it isn't a make-work assignment or one that's motivated by corporate politics.

Never promise more than you can deliver. Be sure, too, you know what you need for the project and what you can expect to get from it, and turn it down if it doesn't meet your needs. If you turn down a project because it's not a good match, do it in a positive, professional way, so the client will feel comfortable considering you for future projects.

Communicate honestly with your client, and make sure he is communicating honestly with you. Don't assume anything; ask, and make sure you get an honest answer. Be prepared, however, to be observant and intuitive. Sometimes you'll need to read between the lines to avoid pitfalls.

If you encounter problems, deal with them immediately. Don't hope they'll go away. If the problem is the client, confront him with authority, but not in an accusatory way.

Learn the art of compromise

In many ways your client is your partner in a project important to you both. But in other key ways your client becomes your opponent. And it's up to you to be sure that you both come out ahead in the deal.

In theory you're working toward the same goal, but you also represent two potentially opposing views on how to meet the goals and expectations. The client may think he knows best, but in reality he doesn't always know best, even about his own company. That's why he hired you, remember? So you need to compromise.

Of course you can't compromise either your professional standards or the success of the project. So in order to come up with a workable compromise and keep the project on track, you have to negotiate. That means you need an effective negotiating style.

Remember, the result of a negotiation will be a compromise of sorts, and that means both parties to the negotiation need to feel they've won something. You need to end with a "win-win" strategy. While the "wins" won't always turn out to be equal, be sure each party can claim a measure of "win." It's important to avoid the disaster a "win-lose" result can bring to your business relationship.

What does it take to be a good negotiator? Good negotiators are proactive; they don't accept the status quo without trying to make it better. They actively try to change situations for the better and go after what they want. The best negotiators do that while finding a way to make their opposite feel good about the result, too.

Stay ahead of the pack

With thousands of consultants setting up shop everyday, you need to stay ahead of the pack. That means keeping on top of developments in your industry and keeping on top of trends and needs and styles in the consulting field. To do that you need to continue to read, study, and most of all, network. You need to meet regularly with other professionals in your field as well as in other fields, seeking out new ideas and ways of doing things, and looking for new and innovative services you can offer clients.

And that means if yours is a home-based business, you have to make a special effort to seek out these professionals. Join professional associations, attend seminars, join community business groups. Make sure you schedule lunches with other professionals regularly, just to get a change of perspective and touch base.

Some people who work at home start to lose contact. They let themselves get buried in the project, behind the desk or computer, and don't make the effort it takes to get out and about. Be sure you don't let that happen to you. Once you start to lose contact with the pulse of your business, you might as well kiss your business goodbye. Your days will be numbered.

And be prepared to be flexible in your business focus. As the needs of your clients change—and you can be sure they will—be prepared to change with them. That's the way to ensure a steady flow of new and former clients to your door.

Remember to enjoy your business

Don't forget why you started on this quest. You picked up this book for one reason or another: Maybe you've just been downsized out of a career you assumed would carry into a well-cushioned retirement. Or maybe you saw the handwriting on the wall as the professionals around you disappeared one by one, along with their desks and chairs—replaced by outside consultants or by yours truly doing the work of two, then three, then . . . you get the picture.

Or maybe your job still appeared quite secure but just didn't provide the challenge or lifestyle you were looking for. Maybe you are simply allergic to being someone else's employee. Perhaps those latent entrepreneurial genes finally burst forth, and you decided to bust out.

No matter what the circumstances, you have a real desire to realize a dream—the dream of starting and operating your very own business, specifically designed to accommodate your personal needs and the needs of prospective clients.

It's your dream. Only you can turn that dream into a reality—a reality that transforms the rest of your life into a profitable, fulfilling adventure. Now it's time to get out there and do it. And in the process, don't forget to cash in on some fun.

Appendix

ADDITIONAL RESOURCES

National Small Business Associations and Organizations

Alliance for Fair Competition
3 Bethesda Metro Center, Suite 1100
Bethesda, MD 20814
(410) 235-7116
Fax: (410) 235-7116
Combats anticompetitive and unfair trade practices by utilities.

American Association for Consumer Benefits
P.O. Box 100279
Fort Worth, TX 76185
(800) 872-8896
Fax: (817) 735-1726
Promotes the availability of medical and other benefits to small
business owners.

American Small Business Association
1800 N. Kent Street, Suite 910
Arlington, VA 22209
(800) 235-3298
Supports legislation favorable to the small business enterprise.

American Woman's Economic Development Corporation
71 Vanderbilt Avenue, 3rd Floor
New York, NY 10169

(212) 692-9100
Fax: (212) 692-9296
Sponsors training and technical assistance programs.

Association of Small Business Development Centers
1313 Farnam, Suite 132
Omaha, NE 68182
(402) 595-2387
Local centers providing advice for those planning to establish a
small business.

BEST Employers Association
4201 Birch Street
Newport Beach, CA 92660
(800) 854-7417
(714) 756-1000
Fax: (714) 553-0883
Provides small independent businesses with managerial, economic,
financial, and sales information helpful for business improvement.

Business Coalition for Fair Competition
1101 King Street
Alexandria, VA 22314
(703) 739-2782
Seeks to eliminate unfair advantages of tax-exempt organizations
that sell and lease products and services in the commercial
marketplace.

Business Market Association
4131 N. Central Expressway, Suite 720
Dallas, TX 75204
(214) 559-3900
Fax: (214) 559-4143
Works to bring large corporate lobbying and benefits to companies
who do not have the workforce to achieve those benefits.

Coalition of Americans to Save the Economy
1100 Connecticut Avenue, N.W., Suite 1200
Washington, DC 20036
(800) 752-4111

Works to protect the rights of small businesses by opposing the practice of national discount store chains demanding that suppliers discontinue the use of independent manufacturer's representatives.

Home Executives National Networking Association
P.O. Box 6223
Bloomingdale, IL 60108
(708) 307-7130
Aims to provide opportunities for personal and professional growth to home-based business owners.

Home Office Association of America
909 Third Avenue, Suite 990
New York, NY 10022
(800) 809-4622
Offers discounts, group health insurance, and a monthly newsletter.

Independent Small Business Employers of America
520 S. Pierce, Suite 224
Mason City, IA 50401
(515) 424-3187
(800) 728-3187
Works to assist members in keeping their businesses profitable by maintaining good employee relations.

International Association for Business Organizations
P.O. Box 30149
Baltimore, MD 21270
(410) 581-1373
Establishes international business training institutions

International Council for Small Business
c/o Jefferson Smurfit Center for Entrepreneurial Studies
St. Louis University
3674 Lindell Boulevard
St. Louis, MO 63108
(314) 658-3896
Fax: (314) 658-3897
Fosters discussion of topics pertaining to small business management.

International Association of Business
701 Highlander Boulevard
Arlington, TX 76015
(817) 465-2922
Fax: (817) 467-5920
Keeps members informed of trends in the business industry.

Mothers' Home Business Network
P.O. Box 423
East Meadow, NY 11554
(516) 997-7394
Offers advice and support services on how to begin a successful
business at home; helps members communicate with others who
have chosen the same career option.

Nation of Ishmael
2696 Ben Hill Road
East Point, GA 30344
(404) 349-1153
Nondenominational religious organization working to improve the
economic, educational, spiritual, and social potential of black com-
munities in the United States.

National Association for Business Organizations
P.O. Box 30149
Baltimore, MD 21270
(410) 581-1373
Represents the interests of small businesses to government and
community organizations on small business affairs.

National Association for the Self-Employed
P.O. Box 612067
Dallas, TX 75261-2067
(800) 551-4446
Acts as a forum for the exchange of ideas.

National Association of Home Based Businesses
P.O. Box 30220
Baltimore, MD 21270
(410) 363-3698
Provides support and development services to home-based businesses.

National Association of Private Enterprise
P.O. Box 612147
Dallas, TX 75261-2147
(817) 428-4236
(800) 223-6273
Fax: (817) 332-4525
Seeks to ensure the continued growth of private enterprise through education, benefits programs, and legislation.

National Business Association
5025 Arapaho, Suite 515
Dallas, TX 75248
(214) 991-5381
(800) 456-0440
Fax: (214) 960-9149
Promotes and assists the growth and development of small businesses.

National Business Owners Association
1200 Eighteenth Street, N.W., Suite 500
Washington, DC 20036
(202) 737-6501
Fax: (202) 737-3909
Promotes the interests of small business.

National Federation of Independent Business
53 Century Boulevard, Suite 300
Nashville, TN 37214
(615) 872-5800
Presents opinions of small and independent business to state and national legislative bodies.

National Small Business Benefits Association
2244 N. Grand Avenue E.
Springfield, IL 62702
(217) 753-2558
Fax: (217) 753-2558
Offers discounts on group dental and life insurance, nationwide paging and travel programs, car rental, fax equipment, office supplies, and cellular phone services.

National Small Business United
1155 Fifteenth Street, N.W., Suite 710
Washington, DC 20005
(202) 293-8830
(800) 345-6728
Fax: (202) 872-8543
Purposes are to promote free enterprise and to foster the birth and
vigorous development of independent small businesses.

Service Corps of Retired Executives Association
409 Third Street, S.W., Suite 5900
Washington, DC 20024
(202) 205-6762
Fax: (202) 205-7636
Volunteer program sponsored by U.S. Small Business Administration in which active and retired businessmen and businesswomen
provide free management assistance to men and women who are
considering starting a small business, encountering problems with
their business, or expanding their business.

Small Business Assistance Center
554 Main Street
P.O. Box 1441
Worcester, MA 01601
(508) 756-3513
Fax: (508) 791-4709
Offers planning and strategy programs to aid businesspersons in
starting, improving, or expanding small businesses.

Small Business Foundation of America
1155 Fifteenth Street, N.W.
Washington, DC 20005
(202) 223-1103
Fax: (202) 872-8543
Charitable organization that raises funds for education about and
research on small businesses.

Small Business Legislative Council
1156 Fifteenth Street, N.W., Suite 510
Washington, DC 20005
(202) 639-8500
Permanent independent coalition of trade and professional associations
that share a common commitment to the future of small business.

Small Business Network
P.O. Box 30149
Baltimore, MD 21270
(410) 581-1373
Provides management and marketing services, business evalua-
tions, and import and export management services.

Small Business Service Bureau
554 Main Street
P.O. Box 1441
Worcester, MA 01601-1441
(508) 756-3513
Fax: (508) 791-4709
Provides national assistance concerning small business group in-
surance, cash flow, taxes, and management problems.

Support Services Alliance
P.O. Box 130
Schoharie, NY 12157-0130
(518) 295-7966
(800) 322-3920
Fax: (518) 295-8556
Provides services and programs such as group purchasing discounts, health coverage, legislative advocacy, and business and
financial support services.

Small Office Home Office Association International
1767 Business Center Drive, Suite 302
Reston, VA 20190
(703) 438-3000
Provides information on insurance programs, leasing services,
business consulting, and discounts on office supplies.

Regional Small Business Associations and Organizations

Alabama
Alabama Small Business Development Center Consortium
University of Alabama at Birmingham
Medical Towers Building 1
Birmingham, AL 35294
(205) 934-7260

Alaska
Alaska Small Business Development Center
University of Alaska Anchorage
430 W. 7th Avenue, Suite 110
Anchorage, AK 99501
(907) 274-7232

Arkansas
Arkansas Small Business Development Center
University of Arkansas at Little Rock
100 S. Main, Suite 410
Little Rock, AR 72201
(501) 324-9043

California
SCORE Chapter 503
1700 E. Florida Avenue
Hemet, CA 92344
(909) 652-4390

California Small Business Development Center Program
Department of Commerce
801 K Street, Suite 1700
Sacramento, CA 95814
(916) 324-5068

Colorado
Colorado Small Business Development Center
Colorado Office of Business Development
1625 Broadway, Suite 1710
Denver, CO 80202
(303) 892-3809

Connecticut
Connecticut Small Business Development Center
University of Connecticut
368 Fairfield Road, U-41, Room 422
Storrs, CT 06269-2041
(203) 486-4135

Delaware
Delaware Small Business Development Center
University of Delaware
Purnell Hall, Suite 5
Newark, DE 19716-2711
(302) 831-2747

District of Columbia
District of Columbia Small Business Development Center
Howard University
6th and Fairmont Street, N.W.
Room 128
Washington, DC 20059
(202) 806-1550

Florida
Florida Small Business Development Association
P.O. Box 8871
Jacksonville, FL 32239
(904) 725-3980

Florida Small Business Development Center Network
University of West Florida
Building 75, Room 231
Pensacola, FL 32514
(904) 474-3016

Georgia
Georgia Small Business Development Center
University of Georgia, Chicopee Complex
1180 E. Broad Street
Athens, GA 30602-5412
(706) 542-5760

Hawaii
Hawaii Small Business Development Center Network
University of Hawaii at Hilo
523 W. Lanikaula Street
Hilo, HI 96720
(808) 933-3515

Idaho
Idaho Small Business Development Center
Boise State University
1910 University Drive,
Boise, ID 83725
(208) 385-1640

Illinois
Illinois Small Business Development Center
Department of Commerce and Community Affairs
620 E. Adams Street, 6th Floor
Springfield, IL 62701
(217) 524-5856

Indiana
Indiana Small Business Development Center
Economic Development Council
1 N. Capitol, Suite 420
Indianapolis, IN 46204
(317) 264-6871

Kokomo Small Business Development Center
106 N. Washington
Kokomo, IN 46901
(317) 457-5301

SCORE Chapter 50
Federal Building, 0130
Ft. Wayne, IN 46802

SCORE Chapter 266
300 N. Michigan Street
South Bend, IN 46601-1239
(219) 282-4350

SCORE Chapter 268
100 N.W. 2nd Street
Old Post Office, Suite 300
Evansville, IN 47708-1202
(812) 421-5879

Iowa
Iowa Small Business Development Center
Iowa State University
137 Lynn Avenue
Ames, IA 50010
(515) 292-6351

Kansas
Kansas Small Business Development Center
Wichita State University
1845 Fairmount
Wichita, KS 67260-0148
(316) 689-3193

Kentucky
Kentucky Small Business Development Center
Center for Business Development
College of Business and Economics
Lexington, KY 40506-0034
(606) 257-7668

SCORE Chapter 75
800 Federal Place, Room 115
Louisville, KY 40201
(502) 582-5976

SCORE Chapter 128
501 Broadway, Room B-36
Paducah, KY 42001
(502) 442-5685

SCORE Chapter 276
1460 Newton Pike
Lexington, KY 40511-1231

Louisiana
Louisiana Small Business Development Center
Northeast Louisiana University College of Business Administration
700 University Avenue
Monroe, LA 71209-6435
(318) 342-5506

Maryland
Maryland Small Business Development Center
Dept. of Economic & Employment Development
217 E. Redwood Street, 10th Floor
Baltimore, MD 21202
(410) 333-6995

SCORE Chapter 34
c/o Federal Information Center
P.O. Box 600
Cumberland, MD 21501-0600

Massachusetts
Massachusetts Small Business Development Center
University of Massachusetts–Amherst
School of Management, Room 205
Amherst, MA 01003
(413) 545-6301

Smaller Business Association of New England
204 2nd Avenue
P.O. Box 9117
Waltham, MA 02254-9117
(617) 890-9070

Michigan
Michigan Association of Small Businessmen
394 W. North Street
Ionia, MI 48846
(616) 527-0281

Michigan Small Business Development Center
2727 2nd Avenue
Detroit, MI 48201
(313) 577-4848

SCORE Chapter 176
2581 I-75 Business Spur
Sault Sainte Marie, MI 49783
(906) 632-3301

Small Business Association of Michigan
P.O. Box 16158
Lansing, MI 48901
(517) 482-8788

Minnesota
Minnesota Small Business Development Center
500 Metro Square
121 7th Place
St. Paul, MN 55101-2146
(612) 297-5770

SCORE Rochester Chapter
220 S. Broadway, Suite 100
Rochester, MN 55904
(507) 288-1122

Mississippi
Mississippi Small Business Development Center
University of Mississippi
Old Chemistry Bldg., Suite 216
University, MS 38677
(601) 232-5001

Missouri
Missouri Small Business Development Center
University of Missouri
300 University Place
Columbia, MO 65211
(314) 882-0344

Montana
Montana Small Business Development Center
Montana Department of Commerce
1424 9th Avenue
Helena, MT 59620
(406) 444-4780

Nebraska
Nebraska Small Business Development Center
University of Nebraska at Omaha
60th and Dodge Streets, CBA Room 407
Omaha, NE 68182
(402) 554-2521

Nevada
Nevada Small Business Development Center
University of Nevada–Reno
College of Business Administration-032, Room 411
Reno, NV 89557-0100
(702) 784-1717

New Hampshire
New Hampshire Small Business Development Center
University of New Hampshire
108 McConnell Hall
Durham, NH 03824
(603) 862-2200

New Jersey
New Jersey Small Business Development Center
Rutgers University Graduate School of Management
180 University Avenue
Newark, NJ 07102
(201) 648-5950

New Mexico
New Mexico Small Business Development Center
Santa Fe Community College
P.O. Box 4187
Santa Fe, NM 87502-4187
(505) 438-1362

New York
New York State Small Business Development Center
State University of New York
SUNY Central Place, S-523
Albany, NY 12246
(518) 443-5398

North Carolina
National Federation of Independent Business, North Carolina Chapter
225 Hillsborough Street, Suite 250
P.O. Box 710
Raleigh, NC 27602-0710
(919) 755-1166

North Carolina Small Business Development Center
University of North Carolina
4509 Creedmoor Road, Suite 201
Raleigh, NC 27612
(919) 571-4154

North Dakota
North Dakota Small Business Development Center
University of North Dakota
118 Gamble Hall
UND, Box 7308
Grand Forks, ND 58202
(701) 777-3700

Ohio
Ohio Small Business Development Center
77 S High Street
PO Box 1001
Columbus, OH 43226
(614) 466-2711

SCORE Chapter 107
200 W. 2nd Street, Room 505
Dayton, OH 45402-1430
(513) 225-2887

SCORE Chapter 383
Marietta College, Thomas Hall
Marietta, OH 45750
(614) 373-0260

Oklahoma
Oklahoma Small Business Development Center
Southeastern Oklahoma State University
P.O. Box 2584, Station A
Durant, OK 74701
(405) 924-0277

Oregon
Oregon Small Business Development Center
Lane Community College
99 W. 10th Avenue, Suite 216
Eugene, OR 97401
(503) 726-2250

Pennsylvania
Pennsylvania Small Business Development Center
The Wharton School, University of Pennsylvania
444 Vance Hall
3733 Spruce Street
Philadelphia, PA 19104-6374
(215) 898-1219

Puerto Rico
Puerto Rico Small Business Development Center
University of Puerto Rico
P.O. Box 5253 College Station
Mayaguez, PR 00681
(809) 834-3590

Rhode Island
Rhode Island Small Business Development Center
Bryant College
1150 Douglas Pike
Smithfield, RI 02917
(401) 232-6111

South Carolina
South Carolina Small Business Development Center
University of South Carolina
1710 College Street
Columbia, SC 29208
(803) 777-4907

South Dakota
South Dakota Small Business Development Center
University of South Dakota
414 E. Clark
Vermilion, SD 57069
(605) 677-5272

Tennessee
SCORE Chapter 68
Federal Bldg., Room 148
167 N. Main Street
Memphis, TN 38103-1816
(901) 544-3588

Tennessee Small Business Development Center
Memphis State University
Bldg. 1, S. Campus
Memphis, TN 38152
(901) 678-2500

Texas
North Texas–Dallas Small Business Development Center
Bill J. Priest Institute for Economic Development
1402 Corinth Street
Dallas, TX 75215
(214) 565-5833

Northwest Texas Small Business Development Center
Texas Tech University
2579 S. Loop 289, Suite 114
Lubbock, TX 79423
(806) 745-3973

University of Houston Small Business Development Center
University of Houston
601 Jefferson, Suite 2330
Houston, TX 77002
(713) 752-8444

UTSA South Texas Border Small Business Development
Center
UTSA Downtown Center
801 S. Bowie Street
San Antonio, TX 78205
(210) 224-0791

Utah
Utah Small Business Development Center
102 W 500 S. Suite 315
Salt Lake City, UT 84101
(801) 581-7905

Vermont
National Federation of Independent Business/Vermont
RR 1, Box 3517
Montpelier, VT 05602
(802) 229-9478

Vermont Small Business Development Center
Vermont Technical College
P.O. Box 422
Randolph, VT 05060
(802) 728-9101

Virgin Islands
Virgin Islands Small Business Development Center
University of the Virgin Islands
P.O. Box 1087
St. Thomas, VI 00804
(809) 776-3206

Virginia
Virginia Small Business Development Center
1021 E Cary Street, 11th Floor
Richmond, VA 23219
(804) 371-8253

Washington
Washington Small Business Development Center
Washington State University
245 Todd Hall
Pullman, WA 99164-4727
(509) 335-1576

West Virginia
SCORE Chapter 377
1012 Main Street
Wheeling, WV 26003-2785

SCORE Chapter 488
522 9th Street
Huntington, WV 25701-2007

West Virginia Small Business Development Center
1115 Virginia Street E.
Charleston, WV 25301
(304) 558-2960

Wisconsin
Wisconsin Small Business Development Center
University of Wisconsin
432 N. Lake Street, Room 423
Madison, WI 53706
(608) 263-7794

Wyoming

Wyoming Small Business Development Center/State Network Office
951 N. Poplar
Casper, WY 82601
(307) 235-4825

Other Sources of Information

The Insurance Information Institute
110 Williams Street, 24th Floor
New York, NY 10038
(212) 669-9206

The Institute of Management Consultants
521 Fifth Avenue, 35th Floor
New York, NY 10175-3598
(212) 697-8262
Fax: (212) 949-6571

Internal Revenue Service, (800) 829-3676, for information and publications, "Business Use of Your Home," and "Expenses for Business Use of Your Home." You can also download this information from the IRS website at http://www.irs.ustreas.gov/forms_pubs/index.html.

Helpful Websites

Microsoft/Smallbiz Partner Forum is a website designed especially for small businesses, brings together relevant information and special offers from a variety of companies, at http://www.microsoft.com/smallbiz. Also call Microsoft's Small Business Hotline at (800) 607-6872.

American Demographic and Marketing Tools covers two Dow Jones magazines filled with consumer and business data, at http://www.marketingtools.com.

Edward Lowe Digital Library offers more than 5,000 documents to help start and run your own business, contributed by business publishers, government agencies, universities and not-for-profit organizations, at http://www.lowe.org/search.htm.

Books for Small Business Entrepreneurs

The shelves of bookstores and libraries are overflowing with excellent books on how to start and manage small businesses. Here's a random, incomplete but potentially useful selection of titles.

Elements of Business

Bangs Jr., David H. *The Business Planning Guide* (Upstart Publishing).

Ibid. *The Cash Flow Control Guide* (Upstart Publishing).

Ibid. *Managing by the Numbers: Financial Essentials for the Growing Business* (Upstart Publishing).

Ibid. *The Market Planning Guide* (Upstart Publishing).

Ibid. *The Personnel Planning Guide* (Upstart Publishing).

Ibid. *The Start Up Guide: A One-Year Plan for Entrepreneurs* (Upstart Publishing).

Davidson, Jeffrey P. *Marketing Sourcebook for Small Business* (John Wiley & Sons).

Dawson, George M. *Borrowing for Your Business* (Upstart Publishing).

De Young, John Edward. *Cases in Small Business Management* (Upstart Publishing).

Dennison, Dell, and Linda Tobey. *The Advertising Handbook: Make a Big Impact With a Small Business Budget* (Self-Counsel Press).

Gaston, Robert J. *Finding Venture Capital for Your Firm* (John Wiley & Sons).

Friedman, Robert. *The Complete Small Business Legal Guide* (Dearborn).

Levinson, Jay Conrad. *Guerrilla Financing* (Houghton Mifflin).

Ibid. *Guerrilla Marketing: Secrets for Making Big Profits from Your Small Business* (Houghton Mifflin).

Nicholas, Ted. *The Complete Guide to Business Agreements* (Dearborn).

Ibid. *How to Form Your Own Corporation Without a Lawyer for Under $75.00* (Dearborn).

Powers, Jacqueline K. *The 21st Century Entrepreneur: How to Start a Retirement Business* (Avon).

Rich, Stanley and David Grumpert. *Business Plans That Win $$$* (Harper & Row).

Sitarz, Daniel. *The Complete Book Of Small Business Legal Forms* (Nova).

Steingold, Fred S. *Legal Guide for Starting and Running a Small Business* (Nolo Press).

Ventura, John. *The Small Business Survival Kit: 101 Troubleshooting Tips for Success* (Dearborn).

Home-Based Business

Antoniak, Michael. *The 21st Century Entrepreneur: How to Start a Home Business* (Avon).

Roberts, Lisa. *How to Raise a Family and a Career Under One Roof* (Bookhaven).

Tiernan, Bernadette. *Start $mart Your Home Based Business* (Simon & Schuster).

Consulting Business

Bellman, Geoffrey M. *The Consultant's Calling: Bringing Who You Are to What You Do* (Jossey-Bass).

Block, Peter. *Flawless Consulting: A Guide to Getting Your Expertise Used* (University Associates).

Bond, William J. *Going Solo: Developing a Home-Based Consulting Business from the Ground Up* (McGraw-Hill).

Brown, Peter C. *Stealing Home: How to Leave Your Job & Become a Successful Consultant* (Crown Pubishing Group).

Carlson, Richard K. *Personal Selling Strategies for Consultants and Professionals* (John Wiley & Sons).

Cohen, William A. *How to Make It Big as a Consultant* (AMACOM).

Cook, Mary. *Consulting on the Side: How to Start a Part-Time Consulting Business While Still Working at Your Full-Time Job* (John Wiley & Sons).

Crockman, Peter, Peter Reynolds, and Bill Evans. *Client-Centered Consulting: Getting Your Expertise Used When You're Not in Charge* (McGraw-Hill).

Goodman, Gary S. *Six-Figure Consulting: How to Have a Great Second Career* (AMACOM).

Gray, Douglas A. *Start & Run a Profitable Consulting Business: A Step-by-Step Business Plan* (Self-Counsel Press).

Greenbaum, Thomas L. *The Consultant's Manual: A Complete Guide to Building a Successful Consulting Practice* (John Wiley & Sons).

Hendricks, Edward D. *The Insider's Guide to Successful Consulting* (Macmillan).

Holtz, Herman R. *The Business Plan Guide for Independent Consultants* (John Wiley & Sons).

Ibid. *The Consultant's Guide to Getting Business on the Internet* (John Wiley & Sons).

Ibid. *How to Succeed as an Independent Consultant* (John Wiley & Sons).

Hoyt, Douglas B. *How to Start and Run a Successful Independent Consulting Business* (NTC Publishing).

Ibid. *Start & Run a Successful Independent Consulting Business* (NTC Publishing).

Karlson, David. *Consulting for Success: A Guide for Prospective Consultants* (Crisp Publishing).

Ibid. and Michael G. Crisp, ed. *Marketing Your Consulting or Professional Services* (Crisp Publishing).

Kelly, Robert E. *Consulting: The Complete Guide to a Profitable Career* (Scribners).

Kintler, David. *Adams Streetwise Consulting* (Adams Medi).

Kishel, Gregory, and Patricia Kishel. *How to Start and Run a Successful Consulting Business* (John Wiley & Sons).

Kubr, Milan. *Management Consulting: A Guide to the Profession* (International Labor Office).

Lewin, Marsha. *The Consultant's Survival Guide* (John Wiley & Sons).

Ibid. *The Overnight Consultant* (John Wiley & Sons).

Nelson, Bob, and Peter Economy. *Consulting for Dummies* (IDG Books Worldwide).

Ramsey, Dan. *The Upstart Guide to Owning and Managing a Consulting Service* (Upstart).

Schiffman, Stephen. *The Consultant's Handbook: How to Start & Develop Your Own Practice* (Adams Publishing).

Shenson, Howard L. *Shenson on Consulting: Success Strategies from the "Consultant's Consultant"* (John Wiley & Sons).

Ibid. and Ted Nicholas. *The Complete Guide to Consulting Success* (Dearborn F).

Ibid. and Jerry R. Wilson. *One Hundred Thirty-eight Quick Ideas to Get More Clients* (John Wiley & Sons).

Tepper, Ron. *Become a Top Consultant: How the Experts Do It* (John Wiley & Sons).

Ibid. *The 10 Hottest Consulting Practices: What They Are, How to Get into Them* (John Wiley & Sons).

Weiss, A. *Million Dollar Consulting: The Professional's Guide to Growing a Practice* (McGraw-Hill).

INDEX

BUILD YOUR OWN BUSINESS LIBRARY

with the

21ST CENTURY ENTREPRENEUR SERIES!

HOW TO START A FREELANCE CONSULTING BUSINESS
Jacqueline K. Powers   79712-7/$12.50 US/$18.50 Can

HOW TO START A BUSINESS WEBSITE
Mike Powers   79713-5/$12.50 US/$18.50 Can

HOW TO OPEN A FRANCHISE BUSINESS
Mike Powers   77912-9/$12.50 US/$16.00 Can

HOW TO OPEN YOUR OWN STORE
Michael Antoniak   77076-8/$12.50 US/$18.50 Can

HOW TO START A HOME BUSINESS
Michael Antoniak   77911-0/$12.50 US/$16.00 Can

HOW TO START A SERVICE BUSINESS
Ben Chant and Melissa Morgan   77077-6/$12.50 US/$15.00 Can

HOW TO START A MAIL ORDER BUSINESS
Mike Powers   78446-7/$12.50 US/$16.50 Can

HOW TO START A RETIREMENT BUSINESS
Jacqueline K. Powers   78447-5/$12.50 US/$16.50 Can